Nora
A Girl From Chadderton

Nora Gregory

Copyright © 2019 Nora Gregory

All rights reserved, including the right to reproduce this book, or portions thereof in any form. No part of this text may be reproduced, transmitted, downloaded, decompiled, reverse engineered, or stored, in any form or introduced into any information storage and retrieval system, in any form or by any means, whether electronic or mechanical without the express written permission of the author.

The views expressed in this work are solely those of the author and do not necessarily reflect the views of the publisher, and the publisher hereby disclaims any responsibility for them.

ISBN: 978-0-244-77349-6

PublishNation
www.publishnation.co.uk

CONTENTS

Chapter One	The Isherwoods	Page	1
Chapter Two	The Logans	Page	19
Chapter Three	The Joneses	Page	46
Chapter Four	The Gregorys	Page	53
Chapter Five	Nora as a Child	Page	73
Chapter Six	Nora the Young Woman	Page	104
Chapter Seven	Nora and Les	Page	119
Chapter Eight	Nora and Ray	Page	131
Chapter Nine	Bournemouth	Page	147

Introduction
by Nora's daughter Gillian

My mum was born Nora Logan on the 13th January 1930 in Chadderton, Lancashire. During the last two years of her life she used an old portable typewriter and recorded as much as she could of her family memoirs. This is the book of her writings. Some of the writing is anecdotal, having been told to her by her own parents and grandparents, but most of the book comprises of her own memories and perceptions of events, and must be accepted as such. It is relatively unedited, and there is some overlap and repetition - but that is how her thoughts were put to paper so I decided to leave 'as is' because I want it to be her voice. She has written the book in places as if she is talking to me, and these comments I have also left in place.

The front cover of the book depicts Nora as a baby, and as a young woman, and an image of Chadderton, the junction of Broadway and Burnley Lane with the Elk Mill in the background. The mill played an important part in Mum's life.

I hope you enjoy reading about her family.

Gillian Wellby (born Gillian Gregory)

A Simplified diagram of my Family Tree

ISHERWOODS	LOGANS	JONES	GREGORYS
Emma m Jimmy Isherwood	George Logan Senior m Sarah Ann	Alfred Jones	The Quaker Gregorys
Sarah Ann —1901— Big George		Alfred Jones m Florence	Ben Gregory M Florence
Little George		Annie Jones b 1902	Ray Gregory b.1927

Nora Logan b. 1930 —1962— Ray Gregory b.1927

Gillian b.1962

Roxanne Jason Daniel

The Isherwoods

The farthest back I can go with this family history is 1851 when my great grandmother was born. Her Christian name was Emma, but her surname before marriage is unknown to me. Emma never went to school. There weren't many schools about at that time. Mostly the schools there were on offer would be for moneyed people. As I understand it, free education was not available, nor was it compulsory. So, Emma could never read or write. As a child no doubt she would have played all the usual games of that period – rolling a hoop, spinning tops, hopscotch, skipping etc.

At that time parents sent their children out to work at an early age to help out financially. Even a few extra pence could make a big difference to a family's living standards. Emma went to work at the age of eight which was not unusual in those days. Her first job was in a coal mine, although not down at the coal face. The children worked above ground. Part of the reason that small children were employed in the coalmines was because they could get into places that adults could not, so much of their day was spent crawling on their hands and knees. I think Emma must have grown quite quickly as she only did this for a year before she went into the cotton mill where she stayed for a number of years. This work would be ill paid, long hours and most unpleasant, but at least she was no longer in the dark! This was the age of the industrial revolution and many factories were springing up all over the North of England, particularly Lancashire for cotton, and Yorkshire for the woollen industry. Emma would now be one of the many women and girls who had exchanged the female working habits of spinning and weaving in their own homes and selling what they made to a 'master', to going out every morning to a factory for fourteen hours a day stood at their machine and then wearily making their way home again to eat, sleep and rise again, probably around 5am and so start another gruelling round of the same. One dare not be late or take a day off for sickness. At ten minutes before the time for the machines to start up, anyone who was not at their post would find their job given to another. There were always people waiting outside the factory gates for just such an opportunity. Even when her first children came along, Emma took them with her into the workplace so she could breast feed. Women normally breast fed for the first twelve months.

She married one James Isherwood (Jimmy). Apparently, Jimmy was quite a good-looking guy. I suppose that's what attracted Emma. He was wiry with tight curly ginger hair. They lived at this time in Walsh St, Chadderton. The Walsh St houses were very small. The lavatory was in the back yard, several people joining at one or two toilets. The houses consisted of one living room with open fireplace containing a fire and coal-fired oven, very small kitchen with slopstone (shallow sink made of stone) and coal fire boiler for washing purposes or any other boiling water necessity, and a tiny pantry for food storage purposes with a marble slab for coolness - the nineteenth century version of a fridge. This kept food reasonably cold and fresh, although they would shop every day or every two or three days, so their food would always be fresh. Upstairs were two small bedrooms and the stairs to these were by the back door which was a stable type door. Two or three steps went up to the front door. There was a small garden at the front contained by iron railings. In this house Emma brought up her family of five children. I don't know how they all fitted in but it was not unusual to have small houses even with big families. They went where they could afford the rent regardless of family size.

This was the period when many houses were being built for the working classes to rent, mostly because the factory owners wanted their workforce to live as close as possible. Of course, they themselves chose to live as far away as possible from their workers in a far better area. It was also easier for the workers not to have to travel so far between work and home (less chance of being late) so everyone benefitted. Consequently, it was always easy to get a house to rent – people were always moving in and out all the time.

Emma and Jimmy had seven children together, although two of them didn't live past infancy – one a boy named Stuart and one a girl named Nora whom I believe I was named after. I believe she died of 'consumption' – the name generally given in those days to infections of the lungs which since those times has been renamed tuberculosis. It was a very common disease in Victorian times and many families lost children to it. Stuart was eating bacon and some of the rind stuck in his throat and all attempts to dislodge it failed. When it became obvious how serious it was becoming the youngest lad, Acorn, was told to run for the doctor and then the doctor would have to walk or perhaps take a carriage to the Isherwood home. This all took time and by the time he arrived it was too late. Ever since I was told about this incident when I was ten years old, I have been wary of bacon rind. Back to their surviving children, their first born was James, then came Mary Elizabeth (later shortened to Mar-Liz - when saying 'our Mar-Liz' it came out as 'Armerliz' and as a child I thought that 'Amerliz' was her name for years) Sarah Ann (shortened to 'Serann'), Ivy, and lastly Acorn. He was born before 1900 and was of an age to be called up for the 1914-18 war. Whilst over in Belgium he was gassed. This affected his lungs and for the rest of his life he was ill and breathless.

Jimmy Isherwood had a good job, being a silversmith but he could not keep off the booze and drank morning and night. He never tipped up his wages to Emma and she was always short of money. He would never admit he got drunk. According to him, no-one was drunk until they had to be wheeled home in a wheelbarrow. So, one night after a heavy session his mates did just that and borrowed a barrow from a local yard and sat Jimmy in it, his legs dangling over the side, and took him home. On arriving at the house, they knocked on the door. When Emma saw the state of him, she would not let him in the house. The mates said to her they had to get the barrow back to the yard so she told them to tip him into the front garden and she left him there until morning.

As well as being on the receiving end of escapades sometimes he was involved in practical jokes on others. Policemen were not treated with the same respect in the 1880's as they are today. Policing then was more localised than it is now - one constable going around his nightly beat. It was also a common occurrence for constables to have a surreptitious pint or two whilst on duty. They used to call in the back entrance of certain pubs where the landlord would have a pint waiting. I suppose it was like a bribe to turn a blind eye to some of the goings on. Not all of the coppers did this, nor did all of the landlords, but in Walsh St there was a pub by the name of 'The Crown' but which was commonly known as 'The Sump Hole'. Why it had this name I do not know. It had a small back yard with a wall of about five feet in height. The landlord would leave a pint of glass of beer on the wall in readiness for when a certain 'bobby' passed by. This particular 'bobby' had for some reason got the locals in a state of annoyance, so Jimmy and his mates decided to have a go at him. They waited for him to go round the back of the pub and then knocked him out with his own truncheon. One of them removed his jacket and helmet and put it on himself and then they proceeded to the fair to mingle with the crowds. They had no end of fun tapping people on the shoulder and telling them to 'move along, please' and generally acting like the caricature of a policeman. Most people saw through it but some fell for it. This carried on until a genuine 'bobby' came along and with others marched them off to the station. I think they were all fined.

When the two sons, James and Acorn, started going to work they had to tip up some of their wages to Emma in order to eat. This of course did not suit, seeing their father was getting away with not paying up. Usually on paydays Jimmy never got home until the pubs closed so if Emma hoped to get any wages from him, she would have to wait outside his place of work and get something off him before he joined his mates in the pub. She wasn't on her own in this. Many men called in at the pub on their way home. So, one night after work finished, before he could get into the local pub, James and Acorn met up with their father, tipped him upside down and let all his wages fall out of his pockets. They then picked it all up and gave it to Emma. They gave him a few shillings for himself but told him this would happen every week unless he gave Emma her housekeeping before going to the pub. Jimmy was most indignant about this ultimatum but he had to go along with it.

In those days it was the custom for the woman of the house to stand at the door wearing a clean 'pinny' (apron), also a starched white mop cap, waiting for her husband to arrive from work on payday, and Emma was no exception to this. If everything was as it should be, all clean and tidy and a meal on the table, then he would hand over her share of his wages which then had to last until next payday. She wouldn't get any more, so it was up to her to spin it out. Some of course were better at this than others and managed to have a bit left over for themselves. I don't know if Emma was one of these but I wouldn't be surprised if she was. Although food was cheap, in times of unemployment there would still be days when bread and dripping was their only meal. Broths and stews made from cheap cuts of meat were usual (although strangely they were more able to afford beef than we can today). The housewives were very good at making meals from nothing. They always made their own bread, having a baking day once a week. Muffins were popular. No refrigerators of course but most houses had a larder with a marble slab which was always cold. There was probably a lot less waste in those days. I can remember visiting my Grandma at her house and the smell of her rich fruit cake. As soon as I stepped through the door, I was enveloped in it. As soon as I had taken off my hat and coat and the grown-ups had settled down, I would be given a slice to eat. Delicious! Sometimes it was fruit cake, sometimes it was Parkin. I never knew a time when I wasn't offered a slice but once Emma came to live at Sarah-Ann's she no longer made any, much to my dismay.

Large families were the norm as we know, but most people could only ever afford four dining chairs. So, to seat everyone round the table, drawers would be taken out of chests and used for seats for younger children. Children of a suitable height would have to stand up to eat. I have had to do this myself on numerous occasions and it is not a comfortable way to eat. During the week the table would be covered in an 'oil cloth' or maybe even newspaper but on special occasions there would be a white cloth.

The drawers were also used as cribs for babies. Usually the houses were built with a large cupboard with drawers underneath so there was never a worry about affording these. Many families did manage to acquire furniture of their own and most of that which is still around today is considered to be of value, being of excellent workmanship and the owners looked after it much better than we do today probably because they only ever expected to buy one lot of furniture during their lifetime. Each piece would be lovingly polished and cared for, as would the cooking range having been black cleaned every payday morning. Also, windows cleaned inside and out.

The fact that they did not have any central heating also helped keep the wood in better condition. There would not be any carpets wall to wall as there is today. Usually the floors were flagged (flagstones) and covered here and there with peg rugs. These rugs were made by the women as a common pastime during the dark winter nights. Old clothes, worn out blankets, in fact anything in the cloth line would be cut into strips and used. A rectangle of canvas would be purchased from the local hardware shop together with a special hook. The cloth was cut into strips of about six inches in length and two inches wide and folded in half. The hook was pushed in from the front of the canvas drawing through a couple of inches of cloth from the front and forming a loop. The hook was then pushed through again this time drawing through the whole of the strip and bringing it through the loop and then pulled tight. This had the effect of knotting the material leaving a nice firm backing. This process would continue as close together as possible to cut out any gaps until the whole of the canvas was filled in. The right side would be looking very untidy but a good pair of scissors was used to trim the strips to a uniform length and hey presto! one very hardwearing, durable rug emerged. Some women were very artistic in the making of these rugs, using various colours to make patterns and very nice they looked, but lots just filled in the canvas as quickly and neatly as they could without any thought to colour or design. Both ways were equally as good, the main object being a rug for a few pence. Every house would have at least one peg rug in each room.

Emma's children went to school because by the time they were of the right age, free education had come into being, although, as yet, not compulsory. But Emma sent all of them to school. They didn't have books to write in but slates, on which they used chalk, and then cleaned it off once they had learned their letters and figures. I think that's about all they actually did learn - the three R's - reading, writing and 'rithmetic.

Mary-Elizabeth, or Mar-Liz, as she was better known, and Ivy, when young women, were apparently great ones for going out enjoying themselves, dancing, skating, the pictures etc and always dressed in the height of fashion. Their mother Emma in her younger days used to wear crinoline skirts.

Mar-Liz was courting a young man by the name of Thomas Whetman. She had a baby by him and christened him Norman Whetman Isherwood. He, (Thomas Whetman) took her to Canada on a farm but she didn't like it. It was a very remote farm, so she came back and settled down again in Chadderton, living with her mother and Ivy. She called herself Mrs Isherwood as it was sinful to have a child out of wedlock. That's what everyone believed. Those were the rules and you were expected to live by them.

Although Mar-Liz and Ivy were the type to enjoy themselves, their sister Sarah Ann was just the opposite. She was an avid reader and liked nothing better than a good book, especially a scary story like 'Maria Marten and the Red Barn' and 'Sweeney Todd the Demon Barber'. I believe I have got my love of reading from her. She continued to be fond of reading until her eyesight failed her.

Norman was born in 1912 or thereabouts and his interest in farming and livestock soon showed itself. On some spare ground opposite Walsh St, where he and his mother lived with Emma and Ivy, he kept a pen with pigs, geese and hens. At Christmastime he used to get a local butcher to kill a pig which he divided between us all. Also, the chickens. The geese he sold. He and his mother always came to either Sarah Ann's house or my mother's house, or sometimes both and for New Year we went to theirs. But more of that later.

When the war was on, Norman ought to have been called up for the army but he was given the choice of that, or a 'Bevan Boy' which meant working in a coal mine. He didn't want to give up any of his livestock which had he chosen the army he would have had to do. So, he chose the 'Bevan boy' option. It was hard work looking after the animals and doing a sixty-hour week in the mines but it was his choice.

When the house in which the four of them lived, Emma, Ivy, Mar-Liz and Norman, finally came to be demolished, Mar-Liz and Norman were offered a council house in Higher House Close, Chadderton. They both hated it even though it was a modern house with all the mod cons that they had never had before. So very soon Norman bought a house in Springhead - an ordinary four room cottage for five hundred pounds. Norman was very happy there. But Norman's mother, who by this time was getting on a bit in years, found the hill exhausting when she had been shopping. Emma and Ivy were also offered a modern council house but instead they chose to live with Sarah Ann and her husband George. I never knew what year Jimmy Isherwood died but it was a long time before his wife. She lived to be 94. What he died of I know not either but I suspect he drank himself to death. When the sons and daughters got married, they also got houses to rent in the Cowhill area so the whole family were close by each other. In fact, James, Emma, Acorn, Mary Elizabeth and Ivy were still living there when the houses were demolished in the sixties or thereabouts. They were considered to be uninhabitable and were supposed to be demolished before WWII but when the war started, they had to have their life extended.

I have mentioned previously that James and Acorn stayed in their houses until they were demolished in the sixties. Sarah Ann however did not. She married George Logan who also lived in the Cowhill area, but soon after marriage they moved away to Lower Victoria Street, which was a better more respectable area, better houses etc. They later moved from there to Victoria Street proper which was another move upwards. When they married, Sarah Ann was five months pregnant and gave birth to a boy whom they christened George, after his father. He was born on the 23rd September 1901. Apparently, he was so small he fitted into a shoe box and the doctor told Sarah Ann to give him the blood of calf's liver to build him up. There were times he was in between life and death but he survived although he was never very big or robust not like his father.

When the house tenanted by Emma and Ivy came to be demolished, Sarah Ann and George suggested they went to live with them in Victoria Street and so they did. They were there until 1945 when Emma died. Then Ivy went to live in Springhead with Mar-Liz and Norman. There were no pensions for old people in those days. Ivy got five shillings per week sick pay to keep herself and her mother. One shilling went to Sarah Ann for washing and cooking and the remaining four shillings went on food. I have seen them when a cup of oxo and two or three cream crackers is all they have had for tea or sometimes a couple of slices of bread with some condensed milk. She could easily have lost her five shillings if she wasn't careful. A sick visitor used to come round to try to catch you out working, and working meant doing anything – housework, knitting, ironing etc. So, you had to sit there idle. They could also look round the house to see if they could find anything to get you to sell to avoid paying the sick pay. At one time they even insisted on women selling their gold wedding rings but eventually that was stopped.

Once Emma and Ivy came to live at Sarah Ann's house, Emma sat in her corner day in. day out. It must have been awfully boring for her. She sat there twiddling her thumbs all day long but she was never put into a workhouse which quite a lot of people were. You may ask why Ivy was on sick pay and not working. She developed rheumatoid arthritis when aged around twenty-seven years old. Her fingers were so drawn up she could hardly use them and they stayed that way for the rest of her working life. She was on sick pay ** until pensions began to be paid in 1945 when after the general election a labour landslide brought in all sorts of reforms. Both Ivy and Emma got fifteen shillings per week between them which must have seemed a fortune after their five shillings. Big George and Sarah Ann also got a pension - one per couple. I think they also were given free tobacco or cigarettes. They also got free medicine on the national health, free dentistry and prescriptions.

** Sick Pay

Sick pay as we know it was almost non-existent then but anyone out of work 'long term' whether due to illness or unemployment had to rely on poor relief which was means tested. Older people or widows in particular such as Emma were expected to be kept by their sons or daughters, each contributing a small amount in keeping with what they could afford. Possibly one of them would have to take the old person into their own home if he or she could no longer afford their own rent. A 'corner' would be allocated and the poor old man or woman would spend the days sitting rocking, no doubt deep in memories of their youth and better days. If there were no sons or daughters (and I suspect this was one of the reasons for large families) there was always the workhouse to fall back on. When applying for poor relief every single item one owned could be taken into account. Sometimes women would be expected to sell their wedding rings before being offered public money or maybe the powers that be would suggest the workhouse. Here they would be fed basic food, enough to prevent starvation, the payment for this being exactly what the name suggests – work. Depending on age and fitness, some would be employed keeping the place clean, others might be in the kitchen preparing the food, or doing needlework keeping the linen in good repair, but no idleness. Being idle in Victorian times was considered a sin, one of the favourite maxims being the 'devil makes mischief for idle hands'. This applied to children as well as adults. When married couples both had to resort to the workhouse, they were separated, men in one building, women and children in another. Because of this separation, old couples preferred to stay on the streets rather than be split apart after forty years or so of marriage because at that age it would be extremely unlikely they would ever have the chance to leave and so never see each other again.

Many of the families who did resort to the workhouse only stayed in until the husband managed to find work again or someone offered to take them in. Sometimes it was just to give themselves a respite from the rigours of life, to gather strength to attack it once more and hope for better days.**

In Ivy's case, when she applied for poor relief, she was awarded the sum of two shillings and sixpence per week to keep herself. She was still living at home with her mother Emma and her sister (Marliz). Of course, one could buy more with that money than one can do now but considering the average wage for a woman in the factory would be about five or six times more it must have been difficult to manage.

One never knew when the sick visitor was likely to call to make sure the sick person was not doing any work, and this included housework, or you could be considered fit to be employed and your money stopped. Because of this Ivy developed a habit of always having a wash, doing her hair and changing into best clothes by two pm and then spending the rest of the afternoon sitting reading or crocheting. A book or piece of crochet work was quickly hidden away should there be a knock at the door. Any housework she did was done mornings only. The authorities certainly made sure there was no scrounging or skiving in those days. You had to be really desperate before you could get anything out of them.

Before Ivy developed arthritis, she did mostly bar work except for a few months on munitions during the first war. Ivy was very keen on crocheting and as a way of making extra money she would crochet for other people, particularly lace edgings for pillow slips and sometimes lacy mats for the dressing table. These items could bring her a few extra shillings over a period of time. Also crochet work was easy to hide. Whenever a knock came to the door, she would push it under her cushion just in case it was the sick visitor. Incidentally it was Ivy who taught me how to crochet, to embroider, and use a sewing machine. Sarah-Ann, my Grandma, taught me how to make 'peg rugs' and my mother taught me knitting. All these things I learned at roughly nine or ten years old. I can still crochet, embroider, knit and use a sewing machine.

Friday night in Cowhill was rent night and those who had spent their rent money, most likely on booze, had to hide away from the rent collector. When they got to the stage where they couldn't hide themselves any longer, they looked around for somewhere else to live far away from Cowhill. There was always a house going somewhere. Then they would get themselves a handcart, pile it with all their belongings and kids and set out for another district. As this was usually done in the dead of night it was called doing a moonlight flit. The following morning when the neighbours found the house empty, they would say 'ah they've done a moonlight' and before long someone else would move into the empty house, themselves doing a moonlight from another area. Another thing that happened during the dead of night was the emptying of water closets. There was no way of disposing of the sewage so the cans were put out on certain nights and a horse and cart and two men came around to pick them up. They emptied the contents of the cans into a large container to take away and leave the empty cans behind. The nickname for the men who did this job was 'midnight mechanics'. I understand the stink in the street was vile the morning after they had been around. Eventually the houses got 'tippler' style sanitation where the contents went straight into sewage pipes so there was no more need for midnight mechanics. This would be about 1900 but Walsh Street had to wait until much later for their conversion. It was all dependent on the landlords and whether they were willing to pay (most of them not).

In Oldham there was for many years the Ramsden family who were pork butchers. They had three shops, a very good business, and were considered to be quite well-off, though not exactly wealthy. Ivy was going out with one of the sons for a time and he wanted to marry her. However, she turned him down, but whether it was because she didn't want him or didn't want marriage itself no-one knew. The family thought she was mad for turning him down. She would have had a much more comfortable lifestyle, but she was adamant so that was that. She stayed a spinster for the rest of her life, looking after her mother. Maybe that was the reason she wouldn't marry and Mar-Liz never married either, although as an unmarried mother she would have been hard pressed in those days to find a fellow who would have her. I don't think anyone worried about love being involved in those days. It was a case of getting married quickly if you fell pregnant and doing what was best for yourself, although Emma didn't do so well, did she? Perhaps it was seeing the results of their parents' marriage, particularly their mother, that put both Ivy and Mar-Liz off marriage completely.

Emma had ten grandchildren altogether. The eldest son James had four children, Ivy, Ronald, James and Jack. Acorn also had four children – Connie, Stuart, Sydney and Kenneth, Sarah-Ann had just the one – Little George - so did Mar-Liz with Norman. All these ten of course were cousins and all of an age to play with each other. In fact, they were never short of playmates. Someone, probably Big George, made a soapbox on pram wheels and a handle to pull it with and they spent hours running each other up and down Walsh St which had a slight incline. Norman and Little George being the youngest got the best out of these happy hours.

When Acorn was a young man, before he was married, and still lived at home with his mother, he was very troublesome to get out of bed in the mornings to go off to work. So, he developed a little trick. He would put his hands inside his shoes and bump them on the bedroom floor. Downstairs this would sound as if he was up and walking about. At least that's what he hoped. But his mother soon tumbled to what he was up to and threatened to make him go to work without any breakfast if he didn't start getting up properly. The men of the house always had their breakfast made for them. Mothers would light the coal fire so the men could get warm on cold winter mornings before leaving home to face the world. If they were short of coal, the fire would then be left to go out and the mother would then suffer in the cold house - and believe me these houses were cold - until it was time to warm up again. As the fire was also used for cooking purposes, there being no other method at that time except for fire, it would have to be lit eventually. The men of this period had a pampered life in comparison with their mothers, wives, sisters, etc, and naturally it was all taken for granted by both men and women. Even the women thought it the right behaviour!

Sometimes Acorn was genuinely unable to get out of bed in the mornings due to bouts of lumbago. When these occurred, his mother had to roll him over face down, cover his back with brown paper, get a fairly warm iron, and iron over the painful muscles. After fifteen or twenty minutes the tension in the muscles would ease off. The pain would disappear and Acorn could get up and go to work. Everyone used to be worried about being late for work in case they got the sack. You only needed to be two minutes late and you could be locked out, but the advent of WWII put a stop to that (also the strength of the unions). Thank goodness things became more civilised afterwards.

Acorn's wife was called May Richards. She came from a Welsh Mining family who moved to Lancashire in the early part of the 20th century when there was no more work available in Wales. She had absolutely no idea about housekeeping, spending far more on food for the family than was necessary. Acorn did not know where his hard-earned money was going. Big George would say it was time 'he knocked some sense into her'. Maybe it was, but you could not tell Acorn. He thought the world of her. After she had her fourth child, Kenneth, she went into a decline and spent most of her time sitting by the window just staring across the street. Connie, the daughter had to look after baby Kenneth and also Acorn. After doing a full day's work in the factory Acorn had to do the cooking, washing, housework, cleaning etc. but he still would not have a word said against her. Nowadays what May suffered would be called post-natal depression but no-one had heard of it then. Some of the family on Acorn's side were of the opinion she was putting it on because she was just lazy. Maybe she was, but if Acorn was willing to accept it who else was to complain?

Emma's eldest son James married a woman by the name of Ada, and there is not much I can say about their family except that their son Ronald was a bit of a loner and had a penchant for cycle rides along Broadway at midnight. This was when he was an adult of course, not as a child.

There seemed to be plenty of excitement going on in Cowhill: murder, suicide, moonlight flits, may-day revels on the ground at the back of 'The Sump 'Ole', And once a year the fair came for a few days – usually in June. All these things played a part in the everyday life of the area.

When news came through that the British forces in Mafeking had been relieved (South Africa, Boer war 1899/1900) everyone came flooding out of their houses spontaneously. They were singing and dancing until the early hours. For music it would have been an out of tune piano, accompanied by a concertina (similar in sound to a piano accordion but much smaller and more round in shape). There was always a piano or two and always someone who could rattle off a tune such as 'Daisy, Daisy', 'Down at the Old Bull and Bush', 'My Old Man said Follow the Van', and 'the Man who Broke the Bank at Monte Carlo'. These were good old pub songs which everyone knew and could sing.

Those who had pianos would open their front doors and let the sound swell into the street joined by the concertina players. Imagine, say, three pianos all playing at the same time, two or three different tunes, each piano in a different pitch. Some tuneless, some with very little, and you've got the idea. But pianos were their only form of music until wind up gramophones came into being, and then records became the recognised way to listen to music in the home. But pianos remained the pubs main attraction.

So, there you have it. Of course, it's all hearsay, I cannot prove any of it, but it has been handed down by members of the family. Sarah-Ann, Big George, Emma. Mar-Liz, Norman, Little George but mostly Ivy. She has given me more information on the Isherwood family than anyone else. I personally believe it all.

There are many other anecdotes handed down by members of the family but, unfortunately, I am unable to remember them all.

Acorn Isherwood

Mary Elizabeth Isherwood

Norman Isherwood

The Logans

(For ease I have added the following information: George Logan known as George Senior had three sons, one of whom was also called George, known as Big George who also had a son called George, and he was known as Little George. Little George is Nora's father. There are TWO Sarah Anns in this section – one married George Logan Senior, and one married Big George. Also, this chapter has much repetition but as there are 'snippets of info' within each section I have included all the writings. (GW)

The Logan family also came from the Cowhill area like the Isherwoods, but whether or not they actually lived in Walsh St I cannot say.

Big George was the middle one of three brothers, the youngest being Andrew and the eldest was William (Willie). As their father was also named George, I will give him the title of George Senior in order to avoid confusion.

George Senior was probably born about the same time as Emma Isherwood (1851) or maybe earlier. His first son William was born about 1873, Big George 1876 and Andrew a few years later. There was a Henry (surname unknown) who at that time fancied a young lady named Sarah Ann but she turned him down preferring to marry George Senior, so Henry asked Sarah Ann's sister Elizabeth instead and was accepted. When he died sometime in the 1910's to 1920's he left twenty thousand pounds which was an enormous amount in those days. Big George always felt his mother should have accepted Henry's proposal thereby bringing the fortune into their side of the family.

Henry's money was made from loans to people who were unable to borrow from legitimate sources. He started by lending to local housewives the sum of one pound and receiving back one pound and a shilling, thus making five per cent interest, which was high interest for the time. Later he graduated to hundreds of pounds at enormous interest rates. As these people were unable to borrow at lower rates, they were only pleased to get what they needed from Henry. Mostly they were business men who needed cash to prop up their commitments. He also used his profits to play the stock market, on which he was very lucky. I can see why Big George was put out over his mother refusing Henry's offer of marriage. He must have felt cheated. The way Henry made his money, except for the stock market, was of course illegal. He had no licence to be a money lender but because he dabbled in stocks and shares, he was able to cover where his money came from. To begin with he was just an ordinary mill worker, but as he became richer, he gave up working altogether at the age of fifty. His motto was that everyone should retire at fifty. Having all this money did bring about one unfortunate aspect. In his later years he became convinced his family were stealing from him. He kept a large amount of money in a box at his home and the only person he trusted to go near it was his nephew 'Little George' (my father) who was in his late teens. "Somebody is taking it from the bottom, hoping I won't notice" Henry used to say and yet he was the only one with a key to the box which he kept upon his person at all times, even in bed. Little George helped him count the money every week on the day he added his pension to it. Little George knew that the money was not decreasing and told him so, but Henry wouldn't have it. So, it would seem that having lots of money can drive you round the bend.

Be that as it may, when Henry died a widower in the late 1920's, it was said that he left over twenty thousand pounds to his son and daughter. Equate that with today's monetary value and it must be in the region of half a million. No wonder Big George was resentful.

George Senior's eldest son William (we called him Uncle Willie) married a woman by the name of Lily, so it was Willie and Lily, and they had four sons. Harvey went to live in Surrey, Bill went to live near London, Clifford stayed in Chadderton and when Lily died, Clifford and his wife Florrie went to live with his father so Florrie could look after both of them together. Harold the youngest also lived in Chadderton in Sylvan St. His wife Effie was a great friend of a girl called Annie Jones and it was through this friendship that Little George met Annie Jones, courted her, and eventually married her. In the mornings they would pass each other on their way to work, she going in one direction to her work place and George in the opposite direction. When they passed with a 'Good Morning' Annie was almost at her mill but George still had a long way to go and was always running because he hated getting up and was usually late. Everyone walked to work in those days – there was no other way and even if there had been no-one wanted to pay a week's tram fare – about a shilling a week, too much out of a week's wage, so it was Shanks's pony for everyone i.e. your own two legs.

Andrew, like Big George only had one child, a son named Wilfred. Wilfred didn't go into the mill like the others. Instead Andrew and his wife Vina put him into an apprenticeship with an electrical firm. It was a much cleaner job and when the apprenticeship finished, much better pay.

At that time people were getting used to having electricity in their houses, especially the younger couples so Wilfred was in demand not only by the firm he worked for, but to do 'foreigners' as well. In fact, after Little George was married and got a council house on the Park Estate, he got Wilfred to put in some plug sockets and a two-way switch on the stairs and in the hall. The council only put one socket in the kitchen and lights in each of the other rooms. Anything else the tenants' had to provide themselves. So, Wilfred did alright financially.

Wilfred married Lillian who was always dressed very smartly She fancied herself a cut above the rest of us and pushed Wilfred into being upwardly mobile. For example, at a time when most working-class people were renting their homes Lillian persuaded Wilfred to save for a deposit on a house (about a hundred pounds for a six hundred pound house) and apply for a mortgage and move into something bigger and better than the rest of the family. All this they did and bought a very nice house with garden on Middleton Road West, not far from Willie's house and there they stayed until both of them died. They also just had one son, Ian, who later went to Canada to join the Royal Canadian Mounted Police (Mounties as they were known).

    Family and friends thought they were mad to buy a house and saddle themselves with a twenty-year mortgage. It was not considered the thing that working class people should do. Lillian got the blame of course, trying to be 'posh' and 'pushing our Wilfred' into a costly exercise. But in the end it was Wilfred and Lillian who reaped the benefits. The working classes at that time could not see the advantage of paying a mortgage for only twenty years, compared to paying rent for the rest of their lives. I think Lillian came from a family more used to owning property than renting it.

    In the days when young George was a baby it was the usual thing to dress both girls and boys in the same clothes until the boys were two or thereabouts. Then they would be shortened – that is put into short trousers until they were ready for leaving school and then they would go into long trousers which they called being 'breeched'. These two landmarks would usually coincide with a birthday or similar if possible and a little celebration would probably take place to commemorate it. I don't know when this practice stopped but as you can see from the photographs it was still in operation when both George and Norman were toddlers.

Little George taught Wilfred how to swim when they were in their early teens. But Wilfred soon outstripped him and became a very fast swimmer, winning prizes and medals. He also became a member of the Chadderton Water Polo team. As for the rest of the Logan family ... I know nothing about Harvey and Bill except that Willie always went for a visit to see them once a year about August. Just Willie, never Lily. I don't know why. Maybe she did not like the travelling. It would seem a long train journey in the thirties from Manchester to London and very tiring.

Clifford married Florrie and they had one daughter whom they christened Thelma. Clifford's main interest was growing chrysanthemums and entering them in shows. He was a member of the Chadderton Chrysanthemum Society. After a few years experience he began to win prizes. The tricky part of growing and showing flowers is to get them perfect for the judges on the day. Sometimes the blooms hadn't reached their peak and had to be brought forward and sometimes they appeared to be peaking too early and needed slowing down. This is where years of experience and knowledge came to the fore. Years later in the 1950's Clifford persuaded his father to sell his house and put some money in with his own. Clifford would borrow from the bank and together they would buy a market garden on the outskirts of Blackpool. He grew tomatoes, lettuce, onions, all salad stuff, and new potatoes and sold it from the house but it was never enough to make a living. So in addition he got a job with the Parks department of Blackpool. He was quite happy with these arrangements as he was outdoors. Clifford couldn't stick working indoors.

His brother Harold was different altogether. He had no ambition whatsoever and worked in the mill all his life from leaving school at fourteen to retiring. I suppose during those times he would have managed to work himself up from 'big piecer' to a fully blown cotton spinner or 'minder' as they were commonly known so he wouldn't be badly off financially. But Harold liked a drink and his father worried about leaving him any money. It was his intention that any money in possession of himself at the time of his demise should be divided between the four of them but he was worried that Harold might drink his share away. He had no such fear regarding the other three. He was sure they would spend their share wisely. Whether or not it worked out that way I cannot say but there we have it as far as Uncle Willie's and Andrew's families are concerned.

So now we will go back to Big George and Sarah Ann Isherwood. As I have already stated they were both from the Cowhill area and knew each other for many years before they got courting and eventually marrying. Their marriage took place on 04 May 1901 and the following September, the 23rd to be exact. Sarah Ann gave birth to a baby boy whom they christened George keeping the name George Logan in the family. Little George was a weakly child.

When Little George was aged three or four his parents moved to Lower Victoria Street. The neighbourhood was more respectable than Walsh Street. The houses were slightly bigger and better. Their ambition was to get into Victoria Street proper. The houses there were more substantial, better amenities and even more respectable, but to get one of these one had to be a member of the conservative club. The con club owned five terraced houses attached to the club. So Big George made himself a member and got his name on the list. It meant waiting until someone either died or moved out. In Big George's case it was six years before a house became available - Number 15. Both Sarah Ann and George were thrilled when they were finally able to move.

This house in keeping with the rest of the terrace had its own private back yard, containing an outside toilet, a large coal place and a gate leading into a long back. Sarah Ann was very proud of all this and would mop and stone the flags (paving slabs) as often as she could. She also had half a dozen flags at the front of her house which she did every Saturday morning. It used to take almost all of the morning as she used to have a gossip with all who passed. When she heard a particularly juicy bit of gossip, she'd come rushing round to us to tell us all about it.

Monday was washday. Big George would light the 'set boiler' with a fire underneath and when the water was hot enough it would be ladled into a dolly tub. The dirty clothes were put in and possed. To make a lather a bar of soap would be cut into small pieces or flaked and swished about. Washing powder did not exist in those days, but 'Rinso' was just coming into being. Extra dirty clothes, like dirty or oily overalls would be laid out on the kitchen table, and scrubbed with a bar of washing soap and a scrubbing brush. Whites had to be boiled in the set boiler.

There would be another dolly tub with cold water in for rinsing, then the mangle would come into play. The clothes were fed through the roller and the handle turned and the water squeezed out and into the tub. Little George, like most children of the day, enjoyed turning the handle for his mother. Once they had squeezed enough water out, the clothes could then be hung out to dry. If the weather was unsuitable, they would put up lines in both rooms and peg the clothes on them. Mondays always had that special smell of wet washing. The day after would be ironing day with flat irons that were put into a red hot fire to heat up. One had to be very careful not to burn the clothes or oneself with these sort of irons, and yet they soon went cold. It was customary to have two on the go, one heating up, and one being used.

As I have already stated Sarah Ann was an avid reader and enjoyed Victorian Melodramas. Her two favourites were 'Maria Marten and the Red Barn' and 'Sweeney Todd the Demon barber'. She read others as well. If she was in the house alone, she would sit by the middle door and leave both front and back doors open. The idea was if someone came in the back door she could dive out the front and vice versa and yet she liked to scare herself. In addition to reading these stories she would visit the Alhambra Theatre in Oldham where plays were put on. Usually she would take Little George with her. On cold winter nights he would be tucked into a thick woolly shawl, all snug and cosy. She never wore a coat, only a thick woolly shawl, of which she had two - one for everyday use and one for best. They covered her head, fastened under her chin, with a brooch around the shoulders and then down almost to her knees over ankle length skirts. I believe they were as warm if not warmer than a coat.

When people went to see plays and later on music hall, it was quite usual to take rotten fruit and cabbages etc to throw at the stage if the players were not up to scratch. Also, if you forgot to bring some you could buy a ha'porth or penn'orth of rotten oranges and tomatoes in the foyer. Once the audience started throwing things the stage manager would come on and drag he or she off and put the next act on.

In his childhood years, Little George became a paperboy, a butcher boy on Saturdays, and sold chocolate bars in the local cinema (five minutes from his home), four evenings a week. This last job was his favourite as it gave him free access to the films shown. The film changed twice a week - Monday Tuesday and Wednesday and then a different one on Thursday Friday and Saturday. No Sunday films then, not until wartime and then it was for morale purposes, so he saw two films per week for free. Naturally he got paid for this work.

As a child at school he was considered to be quite clever and his headmaster wanted him to study to be a teacher but Big George could not afford it at the time, so Little George had to go to work in the cotton mill instead. At the age of twelve, as many did, he went half day school / half day work. This helped to bring home a small amount of money plus keeping up with their education.

Of the three Logan brothers, Andrew the youngest was the first to die. There was a spiritualist church started up in Chadderton and Andrew's wife Vina wanted to go to contact him so she persuaded Sarah Ann to accompany her. At first, she was all for it but after half a dozen sessions she began to feel scared so stopped going. As Vina never heard from Andrew, she also gave up so that was the end of spiritualism for those two.

Sarah Ann and Lily, with George and Willie often went out in a foursome up to Oldham. Where they went, I do not know but I do know they were extremely fashionable clothes-wise. At that time, wearing tight hobble skirts and bustle was the fashion. In fact, when they tried to get on the tram which had a very high step, George and Willie had to stand behind them and push them up. Once on the bus they couldn't sit down because of the bustles so the men sat and the women stood all the way from Chadderton to Oldham.

Pawnbrokers (recognisable by the three balls hung outside) were very much in demand in the early twentieth century and George and Sarah Ann did have to pledge items from time to time.

Best suits or very good shoes or pocket watches (especially gold ones) were the most usual for people to leave.

When Little George was in his early twenties, he and his cousin Harold Logan, and their two mates Harold Lennard and Wilf Bethell, went tent camping on the Isle of Man. Unfortunately, they had torrential rain all week. A year or two later George and Harold Logan took Annie and Effie to the Isle of Man. This time they stayed in boarding houses in Douglas (men in one, girls in another, that's the way it had to be then), If they weren't back in the house by 10.30pm they were locked out, so they asked for a key which eventually after much arguing and cajoling they managed to get.

When Sarah Ann was in her forties, she developed a disease of the gums called Pyorrhoea which at that time was very prevalent due to a lack of dental hygiene. Lots of people contracted it and the only cure was the removal of all one's teeth. A new set of dentures at the time would be eight pounds and Sarah Ann could not afford this all at once so she started to pay two shillings and sixpence per week. After she had almost paid the full price and was expecting new dentures to be fitted the dentist ran off with a woman and took all the money he had collected from his customers with him. She couldn't afford to start again with another dentist so she stayed toothless for the rest of her life, but oh boy could she eat. Being toothless never stopped her from eating or chewing anything.

Little George was still living at home in the twenties. Sons and daughters hardly ever left home until they married and even then they could live at home until they got a house to rent. As houses to rent were easy to come by, except for council houses, this did not take very long. When they left school both boys and girls would give their mother their wages and she in turn would give them pocket money – just a few pennies to spend. This would increase as they got older and earned higher wages. When they became eighteen they usually boarded instead. That is, they arranged a weekly allowance to give to their mother to cover food washing and anything else mother did. Once this was paid the rest was their own. This way of doing things still carried on into the nineteen forties and fifties and I did the same, up until I married in 1949.

Little George's taste in music developed about this time. He bought a wind up gramophone, not a portable, but a free standing one, about the size of a bedding box. Two doors at the front controlled the volume - have both doors wide open and the sound came crashing out, or close them both and it was quiet as a mouse, or open it at various stages in between to get the volume required. The records were big, cumbersome and heavy in those days, big twelve-inch ones. He liked operatic arias, military marches, music hall songs. And a little bit of twenties dance music. He hung onto that gramophone for years, even after the Second World War, but once he bought a radio, he relegated it to upstairs, took out all the innards and made it into a blanket box and it was still in use until he died and I had to sell everything from the house. So I think he got his money's worth from that item.

When Little George was still a child it was customary for a wife to make a dinner for her husband that would then be transported to his place of work at lunchtime by a child of the family. For this little errand the child would have the privilege of being allowed to leave school five minutes early. He didn't dare dawdle on the way with the dinner. Woe-betide him or her if father's dinner was cold on arrival. Usually the dinner would be something in a pudding basin such as stew and dumplings, potato hash, hot pot, cottage pie, all kinds of meals along those lines. The basin would be wrapped in a red kerchief and the four corners tied on top. If the wife worked and was unable to make a dinner for her husband there were quite a number of women who made a living from making meals for other people. If they only made five or six per day with a profit of sixpence on each meal, they made quite a good living, remembering how cheap food was in those days. Nowadays it would never be allowed to make meals in your own kitchen for reasons of hygiene. But I'll bet those meals made over an open fire or a coal fired oven tasted far better than some of the supermarket foods we have today. Only if a man or woman lived very close to his or her workplace could he or she come home at dinnertime otherwise they would expect their dinner brought to them. Sometimes if money was short the women would take sandwiches for themselves instead of a hot meal. Always the men got first choice.

Up until 1914 when the first world war started, all pubs were open from six am until ten pm, but after the start of the war, munition workers were calling in the pubs on their way to work and staying on until they were unfit to do their jobs so the Government decided to close down the pubs from six am until twelve noon and from two-thirty pm till six or seven pm. They could then remain open until ten-thirty pm and ten pm on Sundays. This rule remained until quite recently. It was the Thatcherite years that saw the end of it. There was also another innovation, the 'no treating' rule. When you went to the bar you could only buy one drink for yourself and none for your friends. This did not last long as it made life very difficult for customers and bar staff alike.

Roundabout the year 1926 when Little George would be around twenty-five, he and Annie Jones started courting seriously and they planned to marry in September 1928. However, Annie's youngest brother Arthur at twenty-one had a fatal motorcycle accident at that time. He was in a coma for several weeks and eventually died so they decided to postpone the wedding until January 1929.

The reception was held at the 'Sump 'ole.' Big George wanted him to hold it at the Conservative Club but Little George being a fanatical Labour supporter (and member of the Labour Party although his Father did not know that) would have none of it so the 'sump 'ole' it was. He and Annie came to live with Big George and Sarah Ann. I believe the parents were grateful for the money that George and Annie paid them as just at that time Big George's workplace closed down and he was on the dole then from 1930 until 1939 when the Second World War started. He would be fifty-four in 1930 and sixty-three when he got his next job as night watchman at a cotton factory for the duration of the war. When the war finished, he and Sarah Ann got the better pensions so he wasn't bothered any more about not having any work and he had to admit to his son that the new Labour

Government did more for the pensioner than any Tories of the past.

As soon as Little George and Annie married, Little George put his name down for a council house. He could have rented a four roomed house right opposite his parents' house and that's what Sarah Ann wanted him to do but George wanted something more modern with a bathroom, hot water cistern, electricity and a garden. He knew he might have a long wait but in 1932, two and a half years after their marriage, he got the key to a brand new house on the new Park Estate. He was one of the first tenants on the estate along with his next door neighbours Elson and Ella Jackson. Before being allocated this house, Annie had given birth to a daughter (me) in January 1930 (13th) but as they needed to work in order to pay the rent and bills they asked Little George's parents to look after me Monday to Friday and they would pay them for this and have me at weekends and so it was arranged. As it turned out I lived at my grandparents house for ten years and only went back to live with my parents when I changed schools at age eleven to go to North Chadderton School which was closer to home.

Little George had been too young to join the army in the first war. Instead he had carried on working in the cotton mill, gaining experience and climbing up to a more responsible position until at the tender age of eighteen/nineteen he was treated as a man with the experience and knowledge of an older man – a 'Minder' in fact, who were the 'top dogs' in the spinning room. All the young men who did join the army were promised their jobs would be waiting for them after the war finished should they want them back. Some did want them back, some did not, but due to the number of men killed on the battlefront and also the outbreak of the Spanish Flu which occurred and also killed thousands of people worldwide not enough men came back to the mills, so someone like George regardless of youth was necessary. And so he was kept on as a minder. The next twenty years were not all plain sailing sometimes in full employment, sometimes on the dole, but they got through. When in early 1939 it became obvious another war was on the way George made a decision.

He had been too young for the first war and now at thirty-eight he was too old for the next one so before the government slapped a compulsory work order on the cotton industry (which would mean he could not leave) he went to A.V. Roes aircraft factory and applied for a job. His first job was as a driver's mate on the big lorries, taking aircraft fuselages and wings to Liverpool docks. This they had to do during air raids. It was very scary. Later he got a different job inside the factory, riveting the petrol tanks. He stayed on this throughout the war and earned some very good money. Had he still been a minder in the mill he would have been earning between seven pounds and eight pounds per week which was considered a good wage. As it was, with his bonus, he was taking home sixteen pounds after tax per week. Not that he spent much. He was always a saver, mostly for holidays and Christmas and the house. Most people never had a full week's holiday away until after the war. They went on char-a-banc day trips. Nearly every pub or club ran one at least once a year. Those who wanted to go would pay sixpence or a shilling per week to cover the cost. Before the days of motorised vehicles most trips were taken in horse drawn vehicles and trams. Little George also put quite a bit away for after the war as he knew the war effort and munitions would have to wind down and workers would go back to their original jobs if at all possible.. He got another job at a cotton mill and his wages dropped considerably but as always they got through and survived.

When they first got their council house, they had no furniture to put in it but friends and neighbours rallied round with offers of help. Most of what they were given was too big and clumsy, mostly being Victorian, for a modern house, so although being grateful Annie couldn't wait to buy some modern furniture. Everything had to be bought on HP (hire purchase) where a ten per cent deposit is paid over. The goods are then delivered, the rest on weekly payments for one or two years until fully paid for. This was the accepted way to buy goods for everyone. Their first purchase was a new double bed and mattress, Then a three-piece-suite. After that a modern rubber roller ringer, very much smaller than Sarah Ann's. All the time she had lived with George's parents she had to use Sarah Ann's big mangle so she wasn't having any more of that, thank you very much. The house was already fitted with a gas cooker so that was not necessary to buy. Other things were bought in due course as they became a necessity and the last item, the piece de resistance as you might say was a piano that cost eight times a weeks' wage for George. No-one could play it but he had ideas for his daughter. She would be the one to learn.

There were no cupboards in the kitchen (except for one under the sink) but two open shelves ran around two walls. At least one could see everything on the shelves at a glance. No searching inside cupboards. There was also a pantry for keeping things cool and the coal place was outside. A garden back, front and side made for a lot of hard work but looked lovely in summertime. Lots of people would come walking round the avenues especially on long summer evenings just to admire the gardens. They would stop in front of any they found particularly pleasing discussing the various plants. Sometimes the tenant of the house would lean on the garden gate and have a word or two with them. It was necessary to keep your garden up to scratch or be evicted. That was part of the tenancy agreement. One summer George had a whole garden full of Antirrhinums - Snapdragons as they are better known - all different colours. He was extremely proud of his garden that year. Later he stopped growing bedding plants and concentrated on roses.

(The following text appears to be a repeat of this chapter, but so as not to miss anything out, it has been included.)

Sarah Ann was the oldest of the girls and the only one to marry. She knew George Logan (Big George) several years before they actually married. He and his family lived in the Walsh St area although not that street itself. His brothers were William, who was the oldest, and Andrew the youngest, George being the middle one. William was usually known as Willie, and here I would like to say a word or two about Sarah Ann's name. The same applied here as to Mary Elizabeth. Her two names Sarah Ann ran into one and became 'Sarann'. Also known as 'Arsarann' 'Our Sarah Ann'.

As a girl she had a very elementary education, as did the rest of the family but at least she was able to read and write although I don't think she did much in the way of writing, But being able to sign your name was a big step forward for the poorer classes compared to her mother's day. Reading however was a different thing. Sarann enjoyed reading, especially novelettes. One of her favourites was 'Maria Marten and the Red Barn' which was a typical Victorian melodrama. It was often performed in the theatres (another favourite pastime of Sarann) along with 'Sweeney Todd the demon barber' and others. She was also an avid reader of women's magazines and particularly enjoyed thriller type stories but did not have much time for a slushy romance. I can remember two of these weekly papers she liked were 'The Red Star' and 'The Red Letter' but these were much later in her life, in the late thirties.

Although she had a somewhat nervous disposition, Sarann liked to scare herself. George knew of this and when they were both in their late teens, he would play practical jokes on her. One such was as follows. Knowing she was alone in the house one night, and spying through the curtains to make sure she was deeply interested in the book she was reading he made a cardboard cylinder of a size to fit the end into the bottom of a drainpipe. Taking a deep breath first he then exhaled into the cardboard cylinder. This had the result of reverberating upwards and the noise thus produced was like the roaring of a lion. George did this two or three times and the end result was Sarann came flying out of the house as though the devil was after her. I believe it was a long time before she got to know who was responsible for her fright and how it came about. Sometimes if she was reading something particularly frightening she would place her chair by the door which connected the living room and kitchen thus putting herself right in the centre of the house, The front door and back door, which were in line with where she had chosen to sit, were both then left wide open, (this she did even when it was dark outside) the idea being that should anyone come after her through a door she could make a fast exit through the other one. The neighbours got used to passing her house and seeing this strange phenomenon.

One thing about Sarann was her sense of humour. She could soon see the funny side of any incident and was never afraid to laugh at herself. I well remember in her later years, when I was in my early twenties and living at that time in her house. I came in the back door and found her sitting on top of the gas cooker. She was alone in the house and had been cleaning the kitchen windows, a job which necessitated climbing up on the said gas cooker in order to reach them. Having cleaned them she had got herself into a position where she was unable to get down again. (She was well into her sixties). I was the first person to enter the house since getting herself into this predicament, a matter of well over an hour. One would expect her to be in a bit of state by this time but when I asked her 'what on earth are you doing up there' she just doubled up with laughter which made it an even longer job to get her down. We got her to promise not to clean the kitchen windows unless there was someone else in the house. (It should be noted she was never happy with the standard if anyone else cleaned them and would do them again anyway)

Sarann also enjoyed her food. One of her favourite meals was an old-fashioned meat pudding, that is to say one made with suet pastry and boiled in a rag for about three hours. She particularly liked 'sofa ends' so called because they were thick rolls of suet pastry rather like the fat arms of a sofa, one at each end of the pudding When living at home before her marriage they were all sat down around the kitchen table having a meal such as this when somehow the curtains caught fire. Everyone jumped from their seats to put it out. All except Sarann, who calmly carried on eating. When the fire was put out one of the family calmly remarked that she had not been much help. She replied, 'There was enough of you without me. Besides, my dinner would have gone cold.' A fact the others were too well aware of as their dinners were now stone cold.

In physical appearance Sarann was shorter than her two sisters, who were both fairly tall and slim. All three had dark hair which they got from their mother Emma. Sarann had auburn highlights in her hair, not present in the other two. This must have come from her father Jimmy. The son James had the same colour hair as his father, but without the curls. The other son Acorn was dark, like the girls.

Even when in her seventies Sarann had few grey hairs, and still had a slight natural wave.

The man she married, George Logan, was quite tall, abut 5ft 10, dark-haired and with a full moustache as was the fashion of the day for men. He worked in the engine room of a factory, probably what was known as an 'oiler and greaser'. I do not know a great deal about his background and family. I believe his father was also called George and his mother's name was Sarah Ann, the same as the girl he married. Must have been a popular name at that time.

The son of George and Sarann (Little George) was born on 23rd September 1901. He was premature and very small at birth and a rather sickly baby. He had to be kept warm at all times and so was always well wrapped up. One wonders now if this was the right treatment now knowing the benefits of fresh air and free movement. The doctor also recommended that Sarann take the blood from calf's liver and feed this to him several times a week. I think they mixed it with Oxo and Bovril. I don't think he had it neat!

The liver must have done its job as George survived and thrived and lived until he was seventy-seven. One more month and he would have been seventy-eight. Living as they did in Walsh St there would have been plenty of relatives around to lend a hand with the upbringing of Little George and lots of other children for him to play with for although he was to remain an only child, he was never a lonely one. If we were to see photographs of him (or any other child) taken during the first twelve months of life I doubt we would know if he was a boy or girl. The reason being that all babies were dressed in long robes regardless of sex, for the first year. After this period, they were shortened that is to say the long robes were discontinued and shorter ones, mostly knee length were introduced, but... the boys still wore skirts. The next process in the clothes game was the 'breeching'. Although I have spelt it thus it would have been pronounced 'britching.' This would take place sometime before the boy was due to start infant school. The skirts were now discarded and breeches or short trousers took their place. You will notice I have specified short trousers – boys did not start to wear long trousers until they were fourteen or thereabouts, or when they left school. The business of 'shortening' and 'breeching' were a sort of milestone in a child's life and were treated by the family as an occasion for a get together of the proud grandparents and any other really close relative. They would be invited to tea on the day chosen, usually a Sunday for obvious reasons, perhaps a special cake would be made, and the child would be displayed in his new trappings for all to see and wonder at. I can remember listening to conversations between my grandparents and others of the family when maybe a certain year was to be pinpointed and one would say 'oh yes, that was the year after George was shortened" or perhaps 'I think that happened the year George was breeched', so these events were clearly of much importance to them.

I believe George had a happy childhood. Certainly, from the stories he has related to me it would seem so. As I have previously mentioned he had plenty of company, both of children and adults, and one of these was his Uncle Acorn. Being the youngest of the Isherwoods, Acorn was only about ten years older than George and so spent many an hour pushing him up and down Walsh Street in a wooden bogey. This would be nothing more elaborate than a box with some old pram wheels attached and two long handles. What George liked best was for Acorn or whoever was pushing the contraption to let go of the handles halfway down the street and let the bogey sail down under its momentum. As you can imagine the bogey would gather speed as it forged ahead and George would issue whoops of delight as the bogey raced along. Fortunately, the street levelled out at the bottom which helped to slow him down. His mother however took a dim view of these antics and forbid Acorn and others to give in to George's pleadings, so he only got his way when Sarann was out of earshot.

George also had relatives on his father's side but he did not see a great deal of them until he was older. I have already mentioned Big George's brothers William and Andrew who were of course Little George's uncles. There were cousins also, Harvey, William, Harold and Clifford who were the sons of Uncle Willie and Wilfred who was Andrew's son. Harvey and William (Bill) were both older than George. Harold was about the same age and Clifford and Wilfred both younger. I personally never knew Harvey and Bill. I understand that as adults they married and moved away from the Lancashire area, somewhere in the South of England. Harold, I knew, and also Clifford, but we will come to them later.

Soon after Little George started school, Sarann and Big George got the chance of a house to rent in Lower Victoria Street, still in Chadderton, but about half a mile from Walsh Street. This would have been considered a step up for them and probably the rent would be slightly more than they had been paying in Walsh Street. Perhaps Big George got a raise in his wages? but whatever the reason – they moved. During this period, they purchased the bulk of their furniture which they were to keep right up until the 1950's. Big George became a member of the local Conservative Club which was situated close by, and in addition to weekday school, Little George started to attend the Methodist Sunday school. He was such a regular attender that he was presented with various books at different times as a result of his endeavours. I remember seeing two of these books – one was Uncle Tom's Cabin, which I subsequently read myself, but I cannot remember the other one. No doubt I read that one also as I turned out to be an avid reader myself. Goodness knows what happened to these books but I know he was quite proud of them. The strange thing about this Sunday school business is that he never progressed to being a churchgoer or even a believer. In fact, at one time when I was ten years old, I wanted to start going to St Marks Sunday school but he would not agree to it. Strange...

I have already stated that Sarann liked to visit the theatre and when Little George was old enough, she took him also. They went mostly to a theatre called the Alhambra, which was in Oldham, and necessitated a tram ride (possibly a horse draw tram) where in addition to plays, 'magic lantern' shows were also given. These were the forerunner to moving pictures. The Theatre Royal was another favourite haunt, this time for variety shows, all the stars of the day would play there at some time or another, plus Pantomimes around Christmas time, much the same as today. Little George enjoyed these outings with his mother. He used to mention them to me in later years, especially how he would be tucked under his mother's shawl out of the cold and wet, as they journeyed to and from the theatre. Most working-class women wore shawls in those days, having one shawl for weekdays and one for best. They were quite large, made of wool, and when wrapped around the head they covered everything down to knee level so you can see how Little George got himself tucked underneath. The shawls were fastened under the chin with a very large pin, like a nappy pin, but much bigger and one would have a plain one for every day and a rather fancy one for Sundays. Although eventually shawls went out of use and coats became the normal wear, some older women, and Sarann was one of them, kept her shawl for going out shopping locally, right up to her last days. She did have a coat which she wore if she was going anywhere special.

Her husband 'Big George' was not at all interested in theatres, plays, or magic lanterns. His leisure time was spent mostly in the Conservative club. He liked his beer, and often he had a drop too much, but he was never violent or offensive with it, just a bit silly. He went there most weeknights, without Sarann of course. Women did not frequent pubs or clubs, except a certain type of women who could be found in the seedier pubs of the town. This was true of all big towns and Olham was no exception. I expect there were several of these lowlife places to be found, but as I grew up most of them disappeared. Two were still standing after the Second World War. One was the 'Prince William of Gloucester' better known to all and sundry as 'Top Drum' and another the 'Crown and Anchor'. The latter I went into once to see what it was like, but that's another story. The 'Top Drum' I never saw the inside of, but mention the name to anyone who knew Oldham at all, and they knew of it, such was its reputation. It was situated near a very rough street – West Street – which also had a reputation. No-one in his or her right mind would dream of walking along there unless of course you happened to live there. Fights were commonplace between the residents but woe-betide any strangers who happened along. Then the residents would find themselves in a state of togetherness and turn on the hapless interlopers. Needless to say, with such a reputation not many people ventured there, even the police were not immune and patrolled only in twos. This is not unusual nowadays but then the local bobby had his own beat to cover alone and in the majority of areas this was sufficient.

Eventually West Street was demolished (but not at that time 'Top Drum'). The occupants were re-housed in council houses, modern with bathrooms, inside toilets, gardens, everything they had never had before. The hope was that these facilities would encourage them to live a better life and put their rough ways behind them. It failed. The estate they were moved to – Barrowshaw - soon had one of the roughest reputations around. Shops would not deliver goods there, and couples in dire need of re-housing would not accept a house on the Barrowshaw estate. Later there would be other council estates in Oldham that also developed a similar reputation but Barrowshaw was the first.

There were certain times however when strangers were welcomed in West St and this was when a wrestling match was taking place. They had one or two residents who considered themselves to be the best at this so-called sport and men from other areas who also fancied themselves a bit, also took up the challenge and a 'bout' would be arranged. News would then spread far and wide and all were welcome on that night. Betting, of course, was operative and this is why so many were allowed to come into the street without fear - it was their money they wanted! I don't know if this was illegal or not, but the police apparently kept out of the way, although it was not unknown for some of them that were off duty to turn up in plain clothes as spectators and have a bet on the outcome. Big George used to attend these matches from time to time, especially if he was a mate of the challenger. I hope he did all right with the betting - on that point he was not very informative. I understand that these nights were very noisy affairs, dozens of men in attendance and that in fact there were more fights after the match ended between the local supporters.

Although Sarann would not be expected to accompany her husband on weeknights to the club, Saturdays were another matter. The club generally had entertainment on a Saturday night usually consisting of a female singer, comedian and a novelty act, which could be anything from a juggler to a talking dog. On these nights, women were welcome, in fact positively encouraged, to attend. At this particular club the concerts took place in an upstairs room whereas during the rest of the week only the downstairs rooms and bar were open. This was where the billiards table was, and this was a very popular pastime among the members. Nowadays pubs and clubs always have food to serve, but not then, except perhaps for pickled eggs, so Sarann, who we know was very fond of her food, always took some sandwiches with her, roast beef being her favourite, accompanied by pickled onions. I don't know if she was alone in this or if it was done by other wives. But she wouldn't care either way. There was always an interval so she wouldn't be upsetting anyone when she ate.

Holidays were practically non-existent. I think they only had one full week away as a family and that was at Blackpool but there were often day trips. Sometimes the club would organise these – to Blackpool, Morecombe, Southport. New Brighton etc. The method of transport was the railway, from Werneth Station to the destination. They also had trips by horse drawn open coaches to places nearer home – Heaton Park, Pickmere, Hollingworth Lake were quite popular. This was just before the days of the motorised coaches. Cars were just appearing on the roads but were not very reliable at that time so the idea of travelling as far as Blackpool or Morecombe in a car was met with ridicule. Still, they did manage to get around a bit. Far more than their parents before them.

After a couple of years living in Lower Victoria Street a house became vacant in Victoria Street. This house was next door but one to the conservative club and approximately two hundred yards from their present house. So why move such a short distance? No. It wasn't completely on account of being closer to the source of the liquid refreshment, although I'm sure that did play a small part. The main reason was the amenities of the house. Their present house in Lower Victoria Street was not much unlike the house they had left in Walsh St with communal backyard and lavatories which had to be shared. It did have gaslight which may or may not have been present in the Walsh St house. I think probably at that time they were still using oil lamps there, and both houses had 'slopstones', that is a sink made of stone, long and very shallow. The house in Victoria St not only had a separate backyard with its own lavatory, and coal place, it has its own back gate. There was also a white 'Belfast' sink (deeper than a slopstone} and a set boiler next to it in the kitchen. I think perhaps the kitchen range, that is the fire, hot water and oven, were more modern (for the times) and that the whole house was a lot better and of a higher standard than the present one. Still lit by gas of course but nevertheless a great improvement, and so they moved to No.15 Victoria St which in due course became my place of birth and played a large part in my life.

When I look back on that house, I realise it was a very well-built property. There were five houses in the row, terraced of course, as were all working class houses. Four of them were exactly the same as each other but the one on the end was slightly bigger. Next to this one was a passage which led to the magistrate's court and next to that was Chadderton Police Station. So, they had the Police at one end and the Conservative Club at the other. On Thursday there was a steady stream of men turning into the passageway leading to the courts. Although Sarann lived there for over forty years she never realised until the 1940's the reason why the men were there. When she discovered they were there to pay maintenance money into the court for their estranged wives and families she was suitably shocked. She said "I never knew there were so many couples divorced". Goodness knows what she would think of today's divorce rate.

I should have mentioned Albert Rayner in the Logan epistle. He worked in the same mill as George and they were particularly friendly and always helped each other out in the workplace. His wife's name was Gladys and they had one daughter Eileen who was the same age as me. From us being five years old we all went to Blackpool together for the annual holiday (Oldham wakes as it was known) up until we reached our teens. We shall have more about that when my own pages take shape.

Well I think we have just about come to the end of the Logans until the story of Nora takes over from 1935 onwards and so I will leave it at that and carry on with the history of Annie's family, the Joneses.

Little George Logan

Big George Logan with Sarah Ann    *Big George with Sarah Ann, brother Willie and wife Lily*

The Joneses

When Alfred Jones Senior came to England from South Wales round about the year 1880, he brought with him his three sons one of whom was also named Alfred. This Alfred married Florence, a Lancashire lass, and they settled in the Chadderton area - Nordens, to be precise. They came to England to get work. They were all coalminers. The pits in Wales were closing due to lack of coal. Or the coalmasters were cutting wages. Whatever the reason, Alfred Jones Junior found himself in Nordens, Chadderton with a wife, and soon started what was to be a very large family by anyone's standards. His brothers also married Lancashire lasses and settled in Chadderton and Oldham areas with their own families and I believe this is one reason there are so many Joneses in these areas. The majority of Joneses in Chadderton and Oldham are related in some way if only by marriage.

The first Jones to be born to Alfred and Florence was William (Bill) possibly in 1880/82, second came Alfred, after him came Tom, then Alice, Margaret (Maggie), Annie born 1902 (my mother), Lily, Walter, Hugh, Harold, Norman and lastly Arthur. Bill had 3 sons. Alfred had one daughter - Louise. I don't know if Tom had a family or not. Alice had no children. Maggie had two – James and Annie. Annie had one (me) Lily had two (Harold and Jean) Walter had one daughter (Marian) Hugh had two (Brenda and Kenneth) Harold had no children and Norman had four (Derek, Bill, Norman and Leslie). Arthur had no children.

Looking back, I believe that Tom must have been the black sheep of the family. In Oldham there was a piece of land in the middle of the town known as 'the green'. I think this was once the centre of Oldham when it was nothing but a village. Hundreds of years ago Chadderton was larger than Oldham. During the thirties there were gypsy type caravans arranged around the back wall of The Green', and sometimes when my mother and I went up to Oldham Market on a Saturday afternoon we would see' Uncle Tom' sat upon the steps of one of these caravans. He had a gypsy look about him, being dark skinned and black hair and always wore a trilby hat with the brim pulled down. My mother would go over and have a word with him, nothing much, just 'how are you'. Although sometimes she would give him threepence or sixpence, but always warned me I must never let on to my Dad that we had even seen him let alone given him any money. At that time, I never questioned why he was there (I was only seven or eight) but years later when he moved on from The Green I started to think about it and came to the conclusion he had probably left his wife for a gypsy woman. It seemed the obvious explanation but I never did find out the truth.

Although Alice never had any children of her own, she did a lot of fostering. One boy she took on was in his early teens and she had him until he was well into his thirties and she was unable to look after him anymore and he had to go into a care home. Alice was really upset that he had to be taken away from her. He was like a son and she didn't take on any more after that.

When I was eight, we were invited to the wedding of Alfred's daughter. Louise, and it was then I made a momentous decision. After the ceremony everyone went to Uncle Alfred's house. As the pubs had now opened (I think it was lunchtime) the men decided they would drop into a pub just around the corner. The women of course were expected to stay behind and look after the children, except of course the ones that did not have any. They accompanied their boyfriends or husbands to the pub. I was taking notice of who went and who stayed behind with the children and decided that when I grew up I was not going to be one of those who stayed behind, so therefore I would not be having any children. The ones that stayed behind were also expected to make some sandwiches ready for when the men got back. Years later of course this decision went by the board but I always tried to make sure I wasn't put upon.

Walter's daughter married a son of the 'Heginbotham Tripe family' and they bought a farm close to Blackpool. They had two children, a son and daughter, and the son would have gone into the family business but he threw it up to enter the priesthood. His parents weren't too happy with this arrangement and tried to talk him out of it, but he was adamant. But that was thirty years ago so he might have changed his mind.

Florence, the mother of this large family, died in 1916. It was just at the time when Annie had left school at fourteen. One of the children came home from school and found her on the floor. She had been doing the washing. I suppose most people would say it wasn't surprising after giving birth to twelve children. She died from heart failure and her death meant changes in the running of the household. Alice and Maggie, the two eldest girls had to give up their jobs and look after the men and the younger children, and do all the washing, cooking, cleaning etc for the whole house. They would also be responsible for getting their brothers tin baths full of hot water for when they arrived home from the pit and scrub their backs. Including their father, they would have four baths to fill and then empty whilst making tea at the same time. Who'd be a woman eh? And yet funnily enough they took pride and pleasure in being good household managers. When Annie got to being sixteen, she also would have to take on her share of household duties.

Harold married Ethel and during the thirties, when there was no work going on in the cotton industry they applied for assisted passages to Canada where apparently there was plenty of work available. They settled down well in Ontario, not far from

Niagara Falls and they never came back to England until after they had both retired and then they had two holidays here. They stayed once with George and Annie, and once with Maggie's daughter Annie and her husband Lee. Whilst they lived in Canada, they took their holidays just over the border in America in Atlantic City. Apparently, it was an American version of Blackpool.

Norman committed bigamy, but not purposely. He married Esther first and they had a son Derek. Then she went off and left him with Derek. In order to continue working he had to ask Maggie to look after Derek, which she did, bringing him up with her own two. Sometime later he met Rita and they wanted to marry but divorce was too expensive. At that time there was a view prevalent that should you not hear from or see your spouse within seven years of the wedding date you were a free agent to remarry without declaring your previous marriage. All this of course was untrue but lots of people believed it and were telling Norman to go ahead and marry, which he did. Two or three years later Esther came looking for him because she wanted a divorce so that she could remarry. Of course, now it all had to come out and by this time Rita and Norman now had three children. Rita was upset because she was an unmarried mother. Norman was worried because he had committed bigamy and could go to prison. However, he got away with it. He wasn't sent to prison, just fined. Esther got her divorce. Rita and Norman married legally and that was the end of that little affair.

The youngest of the Jones' family, who was Arthur, died at the age of twenty-one. He bought a motor bike, had an accident, fractured his skull and was in a coma from which he never recovered and eventually died. Annie and George were going to be married in September 1928 but because of Arthur's death they moved the date to January 1929. You might wonder how such a large family managed to fit into an ordinary-sized house. First of all, Alfred got a four bedroomed house to rent close to where they had lived at the start of their married life. The four girls shared a bedroom (two to a bed) three eldest boys in another bedroom, parents plus youngest child in another bedroom and the remainder of boys (five) in largest bedroom. Also, as the eldest boys got married and left home, this freed up the beds and the rooms so I don't suppose there was ever any more than eleven at any one time. They also used truckle beds - these beds were very low and on wheels, and can slide under normal size beds when not in use as beds. The youngest child would always sleep in a cot in the parents' room until the next one came along and then they all moved up a bed. After Arthur there were no others. That would be about 1906/1907. As their mother died in 1916, she had nine or ten years free of child bearing, possibly during or after her menopausal period. That must have been a great relief to her.

After Annie married Little George, she went to live in Victoria St. They had the back bedroom there. It would have seemed quite spacious after sharing with her sisters. I wonder how she got on with her mother-in-law? Sarah Ann was good-hearted – but she was a very critical woman and seemed to delight in finding fault with Annie's modern and 'new-fangled' ideas. But I suppose all mothers of sons are like that. Mothers of daughters too. No-one is good enough for their off-spring.

Twelve months after their marriage in January 1930, the 13th to be exact, Annie gave birth to a daughter whom they christened Nora. It was a toss-up between Gladys (after Albert Rayner's wife) and Nora after Sarah Ann's infant sister who died in infancy. I don't care for either name but of the two I'm glad Nora got the vote.

Long before Annie met Little George, when she was only twenty-one Annie decided to follow the fashion of the day and have all her teeth removed and have dentures fitted. Lots of girls and men were having this done. It avoided contracting pyorrhoea and also it gave you nice white even teeth instead of the yellowing process which was usual at that time. Nobody bothered to clean their teeth in those days. In fact I don't think such a thing as toothpaste existed. George also eventually had dentures but not until he was in his forties, and he hardly ever wore them, except when he was going out and mixing with people. In the house, they stayed in the pot most of the time (although Annie always wore hers) and he could eat much better without them than with. George certainly needed dentures - his natural teeth were brown with tobacco stains and I can remember how horrible they looked and how much better he looked after he had his nice new dentures fitted.

There is not much more I can tell you about the Jones family. I never got to hear much from my mother, except that which I have already written about. Looking back, I wish I had asked more questions. So now we will move onto the Gregorys.

Annie Jones (my mother)

Annie Jones   *Annie with her friend Effie Renard*

The Gregorys

I know very little about The Gregory family in their younger days so I have to rely on information from Raymond, your father, but I will do my best.

Ben Gregory married Florence Whitworth on July 12th 1913 at St. Matthews Church Chadderton. I know that to be correct because I have seen the marriage certificate. Ben lived with his family at 105 Burnley Lane. They, the family, were Quakers. Ben was twenty-four when he married, and Florence twenty-one, and so he would have been born in 1888/89 and Florence in 1885/86 (18th June). After they married, Ben's family disowned him probably because he didn't marry a member of the Quaker cult. Quaker men grew long beards and wore unusual headgear and Ben's father was no exception.

Ray can remember seeing his grandfather in the front garden of 105 Burnley Lane. But although he knew Ray was his grandson, and recognised him, he never spoke or acknowledged him. Married out of the cult you see.

Florence's family were quite poor and as children her two brothers Tommy and Willie had only one pair of trousers between them and had to take it in turns to wear them to play out. Also, they had to take it in turns going to school - one in the morning and one in the afternoon but I don't suppose that bothered them only going half a day. When Florence was a child, they, that is her mother, sister Frances and her two brothers and herself, were so short of money they could not afford food. On these occasions the children would say "Come on Mam, let's go to the workhouse', because there, although they had to work for it, they got a bed for the night, a roof over their heads and hot meals. There were lots of workhouses in those days. They were not prisons and the occupants could leave anytime they wished. If you could get a job and somewhere to live then you would leave, probably until things became bad again. One of the reasons for women and children in particular being in the workhouse was when the husband died first. If his name was on the rent book, the wife may not be able to carry on living in that house, nor being a woman could she take a tenancy in her own name, so she and any children she may have, had to get out and walk the streets and so the need for the workhouse, if no-one would take you in. A hard life for women in those days. Nowadays the benefits system allows everyone to keep their own home and workhouses disappeared in Victorian times.

When it was time for young Florence to start work, she went into service in a large house near Oldham edge. It was very hard work. Up at five am to light all the fires, clean out the grates, prepare breakfast, then there was the cooking, cleaning, washing etc for the family. She wasn't doing it all on her own of course. There was another young girl like herself as well as the cook, and a housekeeper. But this other girl would not sleep in her own room. She was convinced it was haunted and so slept in Florence's room which was against the rules. But she was so terrified. They never saw anything, but every time they went into that room a cold blast of air swept through regardless of temperature in other parts of the house. They couldn't just up and leave until another position came along or they would be out of work and in trouble at home, but eventually they did leave to go into service in a different house. As for time off, they had one half day a week and one full day a month. You wouldn't expect a haunted house on Oldham edge but it seems there were a lot of battles fought there in the past so I suppose it's possible if you believe in that sort of thing. The other girl, Beattie, her name was, became so ill because of her terror she eventually died.

After Florence married that was the end of service for her. They went to live in Duke Street (No.13) and stayed until 1935 when Ben died aged forty-six. I have tried to discover what he died from, but the only one to tell me anything was Auntie Flo who just said stomach trouble. There was no cure and doctors just gave up on him.

Apart from a spell in the army (the medical corps) in the 1914-1918 war, Ben worked in the cotton industry at Fernhurst Mill, from being married until his death in 1935. Ray was only eight when his dad died, so missed out on having a Dad for his younger life. I think he missed not having a male role model, instead he was surrounded by females, five sisters and his mother and I think he would have liked another male (father or brother) in the family.

That's not to say Ray had no rapport with his Dad. On the contrary. Ben did lots of things with him, making and flying kites is one example Ray can remember, but as Ben had to work six days a week there was never time to play with his son, as no doubt he would have liked to. He bought Ray a scooter but Ray fell off and broke his arm. So, Ben got rid of it. Much to the disappointment of Ray. He didn't get another one.

The houses in Duke Street were quite small. Just two up and two down. All the girls slept in one bed and Edith being the eldest was in charge, and when she gave the word, they all turned over at the same time.

Ray spent most of his time over in the grassed area where they built the council houses which eventually we, that is my family, moved into. He was down there at eight in the morning with Lias Grimshaw, or else in their 'pen'. Lias gave him the key to open up the pen anytime he liked and Ray was very proud of this. He would stay out all day, only going home at tea-time, when he got hungry. Funnily enough his mother never worried about him. She knew he'd come home when he'd had enough. Just think if any child was away from home for that length of time – nowadays there would be an outcry and no doubt the Police would be involved, but everything was accepted in those days.

One day he and Eddie Smith, another of his mates, found some privet cuttings, (this was after Park View and the other avenues had been built). They had no idea what they were going to do with them – just chuck 'em away eventually. As they were passing a couple of houses two men asked them if they could buy them off them for a penny a cutting. Of course, the prospect of a few pennies appealed to them so they agreed and these two men we learned many years later turned out to be my Father and his neighbour Elson Jackson. Some years after that, Ray was cutting down the privets he had sold to my Dad in the first place. How's that for coincidence!

Next door to 13 Duke St lived a family called Robinson. Their income came from rag-tatting and selling firewood. They went round with a pony and cart collecting rags from all and sundry and exchanged them for 'donkey stones' used for stoning the flags. The firewood they sold in bundles from the cart. They chopped up the wood to make their bundles in their kitchen and they also kept the pony in the kitchen. Must have been a tight squeeze.

Ray and his sister Melia used to fight all the time. You think Roxanne and Jason were always at each others' throats but according to your Dad they were nothing compared to those two. Ray was always in trouble. One day during the winter he was sliding on ice on a millpond when the ice which was not really thick enough to take his weight broke and Ray went underneath. He managed to get to the side and crawl out but as you can imagine he was absolutely soaking wet. He didn't dare go home in that state so he and his mates sneaked into the boiler room of the mill where it was very hot. He soon dried off. He put his clothes back on and went home as if nothing had happened. Another time he was climbing over the railings of a factory (where he shouldn't have been) and he tore his trousers (new ones) on the railings. Then again, he didn't dare let his mother or sisters see the damage so he had to get home quickly and sew them up. No-one must have spotted his repair cos no-one ever remarked about it.

Near Lias Grimshaw's 'pen' was an old brickyard and one day Ray and his mates collected a few of the bricks on a bogey. As they were passing another 'pen' two old men said 'we could do with some of those bricks. We'll give you one egg per dozen bricks.' So, Ray and his mates started to collect up some bricks. Ray collected three dozen bricks and was given three eggs. He was looking forward to taking them home to his Mam. By this time his hands were quite dirty from handling the bricks so he went to wash his hands in a water tank they had in the 'pen'. Very carefully he put the three eggs on the ground out of the way whilst he washed his hands. He moved forward to get nearer the tank and crunch, a foot on an egg. He nearly cried. Never mind still two left. He stepped backwards and crunch- another egg gone. This time he did cry. Only one egg left after collecting three dozen bricks and pushing the bogey roughly a mile. I expect there were lots more incidents of this kind but no doubt they had been forgotten over the years.

He made himself a rough old scooter which he used to ride down to Chadderton Fold on from Duke Street a distance of two miles and coming back he put this scooter on the bus platform under the stairs. The conductor used to help him on with it. I don't know if he was charged for taking it on the bus or not.

After his father died the family moved from Duke St to Streetbridge. Ray and Melia loved it there - lots of space to play and hills for sledging in the wintertime. When they lived in Streetbridge, Ray, Melia and the other children used to play behind Ray's house. One day they were playing 'house'. Pretend of course and Melia said the windows need cleaning. "I'll do them" pipes up Ray and goes into the shed for the ladders – real ones! He decides he will carry them in the same way that real window cleaners do, with their head sticking through two rungs. Unfortunately, Ray forgot there were two steps to negotiate coming down out of the shed and as he did so the front of the ladders dropped down and hit the floor and as he made contact with the hard ground, he knocked out his front teeth. His mother had to take him to the infirmary in Oldham by bus. She had no telephone to ring for an ambulance so the bus it was, with him yelling and sobbing all the way. He was not more than about eight or nine. He was kept in hospital for two weeks. Why so long I don't know but hospitals used to keep patients for a long time in those days. For example, after having a baby you were kept in for ten days no matter how normal was the birth.

Unfortunately, for the girls who were working, and their mother, it was too far to travel so in the end they had to move again. Edith went with her friend to Birmingham and whilst there she met and married Sam Caffrey. This was just before the war started and they were bombed out at one time. They lost everything and had to come back to Oldham for a spell.

Sam worked on the 'big hammers' in Birmingham to start with but finished up a drayman, that's delivering beer to pubs and clubs and he became alcoholic although you never actually saw him drunk but he preferred booze to food anytime. Edith always made him a Sunday dinner but she knew he would never eat it. When they were together in a pub or club Sam would often fall asleep sitting at the side of Edith so she used to punch him on the jaw to wake him up. Edith could match Sam when it came to a drink or two. When you came back from a drinking session with her you knew you had been on one.

Florence and Ben had six children altogether. The first born was Edith who married Sam Caffrey and they had two children, June and Marian. Next one was Florence. She married Bill Davies and they had two children Audrey and Beryl. Then Marian who married Walter Dunkerley and they too had two children, Patricia and Peter. After Marian there was a gap of four years (only two between each of the others) before Caroline was born. She married Joe Lees but they had no children – whether that was from choice or circumstances I do not know. Next in line was Amelia, (known as Melia) who married Walter Aspinall and they also had two children, two boys Colin and John. Last of all was the only son Raymond who married Jean Hall first and later me.

Florence had an accident in the mill when one of the big leather straps that run on rollers and pulleys broke and hit Flo on her jaw, breaking the jaw and knocking out some of her teeth. She was unconscious of course and had to be rushed to hospital, where she remained for several weeks and then convalescent in Blackpool. During this time, she was paid normal wages and then she was granted seventy-five pounds in compensation. It doesn't sound very much but you have to remember the difference in prices between the 1930's and now. I should imagine the compensation for such an injury these days would be in the thousands. She was already planning marriage to Bill Davies and the compensation money paid for the wedding and setting up home. She needed dentures after this, and this was a problem as her jaw was never in line properly even after all the doctors could do, and no dentist seemed able to give her a good set of dentures, especially the bottom set. If you have noticed her mouth always had a twisted look about it.

Melia also had an accident in the workplace, in the wartime, but hers was of a different type. She had just started work in a munitions factory and on the first day was shown how to operate a milling machine. She immediately chopped off the end of her first finger right hand, so that was the end of her machining days.

When Ray left school at fourteen, he started working for a builder called Harry Buxton. I didn't know him then even though he didn't live very far away. Later on, he went to work in the cotton mill because he could get more money and be on a level with is mates. But it was during this period he learned a lot about the jobs he is able to do today like plumbing, bricklaying, tiling etc. As a child his sisters were always on at him in the street because he was always so dirty. "Make him wash his knees" they would cry and his Mam would reply "Oh leave him alone. He's alright". Ray was three years older than me so it was quite some time before we met each other.

When he was eighteen (1945) he was called up into the army, (Lancashire Fuseliers) and after primary training and embarkation leave, he was dispatched abroad to India where he served for two years. After his two-year service came to an end his mob came home on 'The Georgic', a liner converted to a troop ship. They arrived back in Liverpool and Ray had eight hundred cigarettes with him that he had been saving for his mother and sisters. He had given up smoking in order to save these and as they were duty free issue, he thought he would be safe and not have to pay any duty on them. However, the customs men took four hundred of them away and let him keep four hundred which I suppose was slightly more than the legal issue. He was most annoyed at this turn of events and started smoking again and carried on for years after that.

I have told you that Flo first of all married Bill Davies who also had to go in the army but during the wartime she met another Bill (Bassett). This Bill originally came from Boscombe and his mother, ex-wife and daughter still lived there in Palmerston Road. Before the war, Bill was in the household cavalry, that's on the horses at Horse Guards Parade, Whitehall, where they stand outside on sentry duty for two hours. It's difficult to imagine Bill Bassett on horseback but he wasn't always overweight, only in later years, I believe he was once a strapping young man. When the war broke out, he had to leave the ordinary army corps and at one time was stationed in Oldham. There were many German prisoners in Oldham at that time which had to be guarded and Bill's regiment was one of those chosen for the job.

One night he decided to go into Oldham town centre to have a drink there, and on the same night Flo and her friend decided to go into the same pub. She and Bill met and took a shine to each other and started to see each other even though both were married. Before long, Bill was spending more and more time at Flo's house with her mother and the two girls.

All this time Bill Davies was still in the forces and knew nothing about Flo and Bill Bassett. But there were times he came home unexpectedly in the middle of the night whilst Bill was in bed with Flo. One night in particular he had hardly any warning that the other Bill was coming in and had to make a quick exit via the bathroom window. This must have been a little awkward considering the size of Bill compared to a bathroom window. Naturally, before long, Bill tumbled to what was going on and a divorce ensued. When Bill Bassett was demobbed, he stayed on in Oldham and he and Flo opened a second hand furniture shop in Manchester Street. Later they added antiques to the business. When Ray came home from the army he went to live with Flo and Bill. He didn't want to go back into the building trade so he went on the buses. First of all as a conductor and then he went into the driving school when there was a vacancy. Once he had passed his test he could get his PSV licence and become a fully fledged bus driver. Bill and Flo did very well financially and eventually finished up with three shops in a row. Bill needed someone to do some driving for him - picking up goods from auctions and making deliveries. Ray saved up as much as he could from his wages and eventually bought an old banger of a van with which to do these jobs. It was being self-employed and that's how Ray liked it. He was doing very well until Bill decided to advertise for a 'Young Lady to Help in Antiques Shop' and who should apply but Jean Hall. She was very good looking with red hair and a slim figure and both Bill and Flo were quite taken with her. And as Ray did not have a girlfriend at that time, they encouraged them to get together. But before he knew what had hit him, she was making wedding arrangements and preparing for the two of them to leave Oldham and go working on a farm near Shrewsbury.

The idea of going to work on a farm was because a cottage usually went with the job and so Jean had it all cut and dried, and she could get Ray away from his family.

They were not really all that compatible. Jean was always telling him to take time off work and spend it at home with her. But one cannot do that on a farm. The animals have to be fed and the cows milked at the right time. Another thing was lunchtime when Ray came home for his dinner, she would be sat outside in the sun writing children's fairy stories and no dinner ready. In the end he told her to go back to Oldham, which she did. Ray stayed on at the farm for a while longer, but in the end he went back to Oldham and stayed with Flo and Bill.

As I have previously stated, Bill B's mother and his daughter lived in Boscombe in a rented house and when the landlord decided he wanted to sell it Bill decided he would buy it for them. I understand he paid one thousand pounds for it. This would be in the sixties and as far as I know Jean and her husband are still there today. Do not get this daughter Jean confused with Jean Hall. Eventually both Flo and Bill (D) got divorces. Flo's was free, the army paid for it. But she and Bill B did not marry for quite a long time. Bill, Flo, her mother, Audrey, Beryl and Ray used to all go together on holiday in Bournemouth. Bill always stayed with his family in Palmerston Road. The rest of them in a guest house. Most of their time was spent on the beach and swimming. They usually rented a beach hut but hardly ever went anywhere away from Boscombe. I went with them one year. But it wasn't my type of holiday.

During the 1960's Flo and Bill's three shops had a compulsory purchase order served on them. The council wanted to demolish them for road widening. When this happened the owners never got full value of the property.

By this time Beryl and Audrey had both married. Beryl at the age of sixteen, to Neville Nuttall, who was twenty, and Audrey at twenty to Ron Wood who was twenty-one. Bill and Flo wanted to move to Boscombe and Beryl and Neville wanted to buy a B&B there. Ron and Audrey preferred to stay in Oldham - at least Ron did – I'm not sure about Audrey having been given a choice. So, Flo, Bill, Beryl and Neville arranged to do it together and between them they bought 939 Christchurch Road. Later Bill and Flo bought a house at the top of Stourvale Road, where it joins Seabourne Road. This house was very handy as the back gate of this house was exactly opposite the back gate of Beryl's house making it very easy to access each other.

Whilst they still lived in Oldham, Beryl had adopted a daughter, Deborah. She didn't think she would ever have children of her own as try as they might nothing ever happened. But several years later when she had given up all hope and much to her surprise, she found she was pregnant and gave birth to a son Nigel.

When Ray and I and you came to live here in Boscombe in St James square, Bill, Neville and Ray opened an antiques shop near Pokesdown Station. At this time Bill and Flo had already moved into Stourvale Road. One day she went out shopping and when she got back, she put her key in the door but there seemed to be something stopping the door opening. She looked through the letterbox she saw Bill lying there. She went to the shop for Neville and Ray as fast as she could. They broke the door in but it was too late. It was a heart attack. It wasn't all that unexpected as he had one some years earlier whilst still living in Oldham. So, Bill didn't have much of a retirement.

After having got over the shock of Bill's death, Flo started to go out again. After all she was yet only in her early fifties. One afternoon she sat having a drink outside the Neptune pub down by Boscombe Pier. A man approached her and asked did she mind if he joined her as most of the tables were taken. She said he could sit down and that was her first meeting with Frank Aiano. They continued to see each other regularly and eventually married, I can understand why she remarried – there was a mortgage to pay on the house and she could not afford it on her own even though she got benefit. So she needed to sell up which she did and went to live with Frank in Farcroft Road in Parkstone.

She quite liked it there, close to lots of shops, but too far away from Beryl. When it came to housekeeping money, Frank always reckoned he hadn't been paid. His job was on Sandbanks Ferry, and Flo began to get suspicious of anyone not being paid for months so she went down to the ferry. Frank wasn't there and on making enquiries she discovered he hadn't worked there for months. She faced him with it and he admitted he had left the job months earlier and had been going out every morning as if going to work and then coming home at the right time in the evening. What he did with himself all day goodness knows. Flo agreed to stay with him providing he got another job in the Boscombe area. They sold Farcroft Road house and bought one in Boscombe closer to Beryl. Frank went to work at International Stores Southbourne where Somerfield is now (Now the Co-op) Their house was in Salisbury Road. They stayed there a few years then moved to Springbourne. This move gave them access to cash as they sold Salisbury Road for twenty-seven thousand and bought Stanley Road for twenty thousand. Frank had served in the Royal Navy from being seventeen up until after WWII finished. When King George Vth died, Frank was one of those chosen to pull the gun carriage containing his body. This is considered to be an honour in the forces and he was given a silver commemorative medal. I understand from Flo that as a child he had a hard life, not having any parents and being brought up by relatives who used him as a labourer on their farm which is why he joined the Navy to get away. Also during his time in the Navy he had a mental breakdown so maybe these things explain his attitude. Whatever we may say about Frank he looked after Flo well when she was ill. We cannot fault him on that.

Marian was married to Walter Dunkerley who was in North Africa during the war. One of the Desert Rats. His regiment was captured by Germans and he spent four years in a German POW camp. After he came back, he found it very difficult to settle as did most of the forces who had served abroad, but eventually he did, going back to his old job in the cotton industry.

In the 1950's, Carol and Joe Lees had two great friends – Bill and Rona Bradley. Bill was in the used car business opposite Flo and Bill's shops. For some reason, of which I have no idea, Bill and Rona decided to sell up and go to South Africa and try their luck in some sort of business over there. Joe and Carol decided to go with them. And so off they all went. Once over there Marian was getting letters back about what a great lifestyle it was out there. Carol had a black girl called Abigail who did all the housework whilst Carol and Rona went playing tennis and socialising generally. Back in Oldham there was an advert in the paper for workers in the cotton industry to apply for jobs out in South Africa. Walter Dunkerley applied and with his qualifications was accepted as a carder (a technical supervisor) doing the same job as he was doing in Oldham. A house came with the job and a servant. So Marian was looking forward to her move.

Their son Peter being only six years old naturally went with them but Pat who was now in her late teens and pregnant stayed behind in Oldham, married Barry Firth, the father of her baby and gave birth to Gina.

Marian enjoyed life in South Africa. Who wouldn't under the circumstances? But after three years it all came to an end.

Whether it was the employers who terminated the contract or whether Walter decided not to renew I cannot say but whatever happened they came back to England. Whilst out there Joe Lees had a cerebral haemorrhage. There was no free health service out there and one needed to have health insurance in order to get any treatment. Fortunately for Joe and Carol the firm Joe was employed by had employee insurance for hospitalisation so Joe was able to be accepted by a hospital. If you could not prove the ability to pay you were not accepted. Joe did not recover and died in hospital. Carol was expecting to have to return to Oldham now that Joe was gone as she could not afford to support herself. She had at one time worked in a large department store but the pay was not enough to keep the house going. Now that Joe had gone, the house had to be given up. Luckily for Carol they had a very good friend called Stan Rose. It was he that had got Joe his job in the first place. He persuaded Carol to stay on in South Africa. He obviously had a soft spot for her and even after her friends Rona and Bill Bradley left South Africa to return to England she still stayed on. Stan had a very good position as a lecturer for the Shell Oil Company. He also had a lovely house with a swimming pool. I am not surprised he wanted Carol to stay on and marry him. Carol was very good looking and had a very good figure. Some used to say she looked like a film star. After marrying Stan, she had an even better life than before. They had a boat, went fishing, sailing, bowling, all the sort of things you only expect from the wealthy so Stan must have had quite a lot of money or at least a very good income.

In the meantime, Walter and Marian had come back to England and gone to live with Marian's mother until they bought a house in Tamworth Street and Pat and Gina went to live with them. By this time Barry and Pat had divorced. Soon afterwards Walter decided he would try South Africa again although this time under his own steam. The idea was that he would work at his old job. He did not expect any problems finding employment.

He would send money to Marian to keep up the mortgage repayments and for housekeeping and bills. For a time, this went very well. Then the payments started to dry up. Eventually Marian could no longer keep up with the mortgage. She got into financial difficulties and although she wrote to Carol to see if she could help locate him but Carol had no idea where she was either. So, in the end Marian had to give up the house and apply for a council house which she got on the Limeside estate, Rowantree Road to be exact. I think you will remember it Gillian. You went there often enough to play with Gina. We used to call it the Land of Nod because nearly every time we went there, they were usually asleep in bed. After Pat divorced Barry, she met Ron Spicer and eventually married him. They then bought a bungalow in Knowle St, Hollinwood, and she Ron and Gina, along with a few cats, went to live there. Peter joined the army for a spell but he didn't like it so got his mother to buy him out. So now there was only Marian and Peter living in Rowantree Road.

Marian had given up on ever hearing from Walter again, and having met up with an old flame from the wartime days when both of them worked in the same munitions factory they had been seeing quite a bit of each other. Harold, as was his name, landed a good job on the Isle of Man and asked Marian if she would go out there with him. She agreed she would but it was not to be.
One evening, one of Harold's sons turned up to say that Harold was dead. He had gone home the previous night, switched on the gas fire and somehow the flame had gone out but the gas had stayed on. Harold was lain on the bed all night with the gas on at full but not lit. By morning he was dead. There was an inquest of course. I think the result was accidental death or death by misadventure, So Marian never got her new life on the Isle of Man.

It was definitely not suicide as he was looking forward to a new life with Marian. Marian did eventually get some news regarding Walter. He was killed in a crash with a bus which was being driven on the wrong side of the road by a native driver. She got compensation money for this (about five thousand pounds) and she used this to buy a house for herself and Peter and his new wife. Walter was driving a lorry in the crash. I understand he was also drinking a lot at this time.

The girl Peter married – I think her name was Tracy - came from a very rough and ready family and she was a very violent person. She was always breaking windows and glass doors, anything that was breakable, she would break it. We didn't go to the wedding because we were living down here in Boscombe at that time but we had a blow by blow account of it from Colin who was absolutely amazed at the behaviour. It was a buffet and some of the guests would call out 'chuck us a sandwich, would you?" and they meant literally. Soon there were sarnies and rolls flying all over the place. and bouncing off the walls. It rather shook Peter's side of the family. Although I believe Peter was becoming like them at that point. This was around the time that Marian met up with Toby. Also, your Dad had gone back to Oldham to open up a second-hand furniture shop once more about which I will write more of in Part Five. They more or less met in the shop as Marian used to sit in there when Dad was at an auction and she also made him dinners sometimes. Toby supposedly took a fancy to Marian but it was really her pension book he was interested in. Then he got into telling Ray how to run his business. Which did not go down well with Ray as you can imagine. Also, Peter's wife started coming in moaning about Peter and Marian and shouting the odds. So he had to order her out as well. All in all he didn't have such a good time up there.

Marian and Toby married and went to live in his house in Seymour Street, Hollinwood. Toby had originally come from Folkestone to Oldham and brought with him two old ladies who he reckoned to be looking after but it was their pension books he was really looking after. I cannot understand why Marian married him. It was she who got the job of looking after the two of them. Eventually when the old ladies became ill, they had to go into hospital and as far as we know they both died there. Not at the same time. There was some distance between the two deaths. After the old ladies died and Marian and Toby were on their own, the house came up for demolition and so the council moved them to another house in Elm St. Failsworth. (This was also due for demolition in the not too distant future). Whilst living there Toby had a fall, hurt his head, as a result of which he died. Marian was then moved to a bungalow in Recreation Rd. She was there for a few years but she became a little bit mentally unstable, doing things like leaving the gas cooker on and leaving lights on, putting milk in the kettle and leaving the pan on too long. From this bungalow she was moved to a residential home on Queens Road. Oldham, close to Alexandra Park, and there she saw out her days which were many in number. I cannot remember which year she died or even from what she died but I know she was in a wheelchair for her later years and when she had visitors, she hardly spoke to them, not even Pat or Gina. We went to see her once soon after she moved in. Fortunately, she was quite perky then, and had a lot to say.

Of all the family the first one to die was Edith in Birmingham. She had breast cancer and may not have died if she had gone to the doctor as soon as she discovered a lump but she didn't and only managed another twelve months of life. Their mother also died of cancer. Hers was cancer of the liver. Carol came over from South Africa when she knew there was no hope for her mother. She stayed at Melia's until the funeral was over.

Melia had much tragedy in her life. She had two sons as you know Colin and John. The younger one John was out on his motorbike one day, had an accident, and was killed instantly. Very sad. A few years after the death of young John, her husband

Walter died after being ill for some time. I'm not sure what he died of but I did hear the word dropsy mentioned, which I think is something to do with kidney troubles, but I cannot say for sure. Melia got married again some years later. His name was Gordon. I never met him so cannot say what kind of person he was. They went to Yugoslavia for their honeymoon and a couple of weeks after they had returned, he went to the local pub, the Duke of York, for a dinnertime drink. After returning he went upstairs for a lie-down. Melia was downstairs and suddenly heard a bump. She went upstairs to investigate and there was Gordon lying on the floor. She sent for an ambulance but I think it was a heart attack. They took him to hospital but he died there. So that was three tragedies in her life. She never met anyone else after that.

Although Marian was the next to die, we don't know if she had cancer or not. Flo's death was due to ovarian cancer. No doubt you will remember the weeks leading up to it. At the time of writing we are not sure of Carol's state of health apart from Parkinson's disease. Melia also had cancer. Hers was in the spine like Pat. In Melia's case she had not been well for some time and although she had been having tests etc the doctors did not seem to be able to find out what was wrong. She could hardly lift her head up. Eventually the doctors told Colin and Ann it was cancer. Colin did not want his mother to know. Ann always phoned Melia at ten am every morning to check she was okay but one morning she did not answer. Ann phoned Colin who was on his way to Worcester. He told Ann to ask two of his employees to go round to the house and break in if necessary. On arriving they found Melia curled up in a heap at the bottom of the stairs. She had fallen. She told them she had been there for hours. An ambulance was sent for and she was taken to hospital. She became paralysed from the neck down and could not move a muscle. She was not in hospital very long before she died. Colin put on a good funeral and insisted we come up from

Bournemouth. He suggested we stay in Melia's house. Which we did and when we got there, there was an envelope on the kitchen worktop containing a hundred and fifty pounds in cash and a note which read 'please accept this for your expenses. We are so pleased you took the trouble to come.' We tried to give it back to him but he was having none of it.

Your dad also had cancer when he was seventy, (prostate cancer). He had the operation for it and so far it has not returned. Let us hope it never does. So out of seven members of the same family, five have had cancer although only four have actually died from it so I hope you will all be very careful and diligent with yourselves in the future and if anything seems wrong get yourself off to the doctor straightaway. Also don't smoke. It is the most stupid thing you can do is smoke when there is a history of cancer in the family.

So, there we have come to an end of the Gregory family for the time being.

Ben and Florence and girls Edith and Florence

Carol, Ray, Florence and Melia

Nora as a Child

Pre-School

Very few people are able to remember anything before they were five years old and so this is the case with me. Some of the incidents I am about to describe I am not sure if I actually do remember them or they have been passed on by word of mouth by my parents or grandparents. I know I had a bad temper and loved to throw things at people if they annoyed me. I had one of those three wheeled fairy cycles and when I was in a bad mood I would ride it up to the wall and let the front wheel hit the skirting board with a bump. I think I eventually removed most of the paint from that particular skirting board. Another time my Auntie Lily came to visit us and I was playing with my doll and pram. Auntie bent over the pram handle saying 'oh what a lovely baby you've got Nora'. My reply to that was to 'scream like blue murder' was how it was described to me, and to shout at her to take her hands off my pram. "Don't touch it, don't touch it!' I yelled over and over again. Of course, I got into trouble for it but she never did it again.

Quite often on Sundays we would be invited to tea at Albert and Gladys Rayner's house. I used to enjoy going there because they had a little girl called Eileen and she had a lovely dolls house. I always wanted a dolls house but no matter how long I pestered them, my parents would not get me one. When we went there, we always went the same way down Peel St. and along Walsh St. However, one Sunday we were asked by my Grandma to leave a note at Dr McKinnon's surgery asking him to call in on her mother the following day. This meant going a slightly different route going past Peel St and not turning into it. My parents didn't see any problem but they had reckoned without me. Well of course I didn't understand why we were going a different way, although they did try to explain it to me. But me being me I was having none of this. I was going the usual way down Peel St and they couldn't get me to budge. I kicked and screamed and caused so much embarrassment that in the end my father picked me up and tried to carry me but I kicked so much he had to put me down again.

When they had had enough of my tantrums, I got a good smack which started me yelling at the top of my voice and people were beginning to stare. They solved the problem by my mother and I going our usual way (via Peel St) and my Dad going along Middleton Road to the surgery, delivering the note and meeting up with us at the Rayner's house. When my dad explained to Albert and Gladys why we had arrived separately he did nothing but laugh about it. These incidents will no doubt show you what an angelic child I was.

One more incident I must tell you about happened the Christmas before my sixth birthday. My mother and I had spotted a pattern in a magazine for a child's dress made from crepe paper with frills for the skirt. I took a fancy to it so my mother bought some pink and some green paper and set about making it.

Grandma was having a few relatives from the Isherwood family coming on Christmas day and the idea was that I would wear this dress and 'entertain' the company who consisted of Ivy, her mother, who was my great grandma, my mum and dad, Acorn and his wife May, his two sons Stuart and Sidney who were seventeen and nineteen, and Mar-liz and Norman. I was allowed to stay up later than usual so that I could sing my song about nine pm. I would expect most of them would be ready to leave after that, entertainment notwithstanding.

I sang my first song, (I can't remember what it was but I cannot sing a note in tune so it hardly matters) and whilst singing I noticed that Stuart did not appear to be listening. He was doing a word puzzle.

I said something like 'You're not listening to me."

"Yes I am." he says.

"No, you're not. You're doing that puzzle, put it down and listen to my singing."

I could see most of them were having a little smile to themselves and I was beginning to get enraged with Stuart.

Someone said "For heaven's sake Stuart, listen to her sing or she'll have us here all night."

I didn't know who said it but I thought it was Sidney so I started to throw things at him. Next thing I knew I'm being carried off to bed in a terrible temper. I cried myself to sleep with anger that night. I always cried when I was angry or in a rage. Everything had gone wrong. My entertainment had not turned out as I expected. I was never asked to sing again.

My Grandad must have been a very patient man. He was out of work when I was born (until 1939) and I spent a lot of time with him. I am told he would sit in his rocking chair and allow me to bandage him all over – his face, chest, arms hands etc.

He took me out a lot, too. Up to Greenfield on the bus (in the summertime naturally) It was lovely up there. Sometimes he and Uncle Willie would be asked to do a clearing job for builders, that is clearing away shrubbery and suchlike with saws and axes, and he would take me with him. I was only too happy to play on my own while they were working.

Usually my Grandma would put sandwiches up for dinnertime and a bottle of 'pop' to drink. I would collect big bunches of bluebells and take them home for Grandma and she would put them in large jam jars.

Schooldays

I started school in September 1934 and right away I had troubles. Not with my lessons. On the contrary. I was a quick learner and managed to remember most of what I was taught and soon became top of the class. It was other children that caused me issues, but more of that later. The first year was taken up with learning the alphabet and times tables. We all shouted them out together and it sounded like a right old rabble. When we moved up into the next class, we were taught easy sums and learned to read and write simple words. We were given cards that covered the story of Peter Pan, ten in all, and each Friday we had to go to Miss Sanderson and read out aloud one of these cards correctly until we had got through them all. On completion we got a brand new penny, and the opportunity from then on to read from any book in the classroom. I was going along fine until I came to the word 'ocean' which I pronounced 'okeean'. Miss Sanderson was very patient and kept on pronouncing it for me but every Friday it still came out 'okeean'. I was concerned about not getting my nice new penny but more so, I wanted to progress up to reading any book in the class. It seemed to take ages to get past this 'okeean' business but it was probably only three Fridays. Once I had got it, I never looked back and eventually became the best reader in the whole school. This may sound boastful but it is not. I am merely stating facts.

The troubles I had at school were mostly with other children, especially boys. They terrified me. There was one boy in particular, Jack Harrison, who was one of the biggest bullies I have ever come across. I tried to avoid him as much as I could. He would chase me around the playground at playtime before the bell went, so much so that I began to stay in the girls toilets at these times and lock myself in. I would stay there until the bell rang and then stroll nonchalantly out. He used to do his best to annoy me in the classroom at times, even though the teacher was there. On Friday afternoons, for the last hour we were allowed to play with anything we liked. The boys would usually choose Meccano, and the girls plasticine or corkwork. Jack Harrison always had to spoil whatever I was doing and one Friday I really lost my temper with him and forgot about being scared. As he reached over from his side of the table to pick up my plasticine models and ruin them, I grabbed his arm and hand and pushed him in the chest with my other hand and up-ended the table on top of him. I, too, finished up on top of him pummelling his chest and kicking his legs with my feet. With my two hands I literally boxed his ears. Miss Sanderson came rushing over to drag me off. She had never seen me in that state before, neither I think had anyone else. Mr Rogers the headmaster was sent for, to survey the damage, not only to Jack Harrison but to the Meccano set and the table. Needless to say, a letter had to be sent to my parents from school who gave me a good old telling off but I don't think they understood what it was like for me and the bullyboys. One thing I can say about this incident is I really enjoyed it. Never again did Jack Harrison come anywhere near me. There was another lad, Travis Seamark, who was also a bully. Whenever my Grandma sent me on an errand to the local shops I used to have to look to see if he was about before going on the main road because if he was, he would take the money off me. I had to think up all sorts of excuses as to why I had come back without the goods but for some reason I was too scared to tell them the truth, but after seeing what happened to Jack Harrison, Travis Seamark left me alone. All the same I was glad when he and his family moved to another area away from Chadderton. Some years later when we were both in our teens I met up with him in Oldham and much to my amazement he asked me for a date. Ernest Stringer was another who used to bully me and my friend Elsie. Whenever we played with our skipping rope he would come along and deliberately tangle himself up in the rope so we couldn't skip any more. To begin with we used to run away but then we started to stand our ground and eventually I put him on the floor and boxed his ears as I had done with Jack Harrison. I ran home crying but unfortunately he wore glasses and I had broken them. His mother came out of the house, shouted at me and took me down to my own house and showed my father what I had done, broken glasses and bleeding cheekbone. More trouble for me of course, but it was worth it.

My childhood food

My Grandma was a very good cook and I loved the dinners she used to make. It was nearly always the same on each day of the week for instance Mondays was fried potato scallops. Tuesday was cheese and onion pie. Wednesday was something from the chippy, a bean or pea mixture. Thursday was meat pudding, Friday vegetable pie from the local confectionery shop, Saturday sausage and mash, Sunday roast beef or pork or lamb with all the trimmings.

The reason for Monday being the day for fried potato scallops which were quick and easy to make was because it was washday and my Grandma liked to be finished before lunchtime if she could.

Of course, once war started and rationing came into place things like meat puddings and meat pies went by the board. To vary this weekly menu sometimes potato hash would replace one of the meals. This was cheap and only required a small amount of minced beef to make a tasty meal. There were no onions in the shops so leeks had to take their place.

Whilst we are on the subject of food, I should tell you of the potato pie suppers that the Salvation Army used to put on occasions. Whenever these were on my Grandma always used to take me. They were free I think or at least very cheap. When we arrived in the hall, we first sang hymns (singing for your supper

I suppose) and then we all sat round a large table, were given a plate and a spoon and someone came round with a large dish containing the potato pie which was dished out onto your plate. After we had all eaten another hymn was sung and then we could all go home. Sometimes stew and dumplings was substituted for a change, but there again when the war was on these things had to change and they came to an end. I don't think they started up again after the war. Lots of things that had been popular before the war started, we never saw again.

As I have mentioned, we had pea or bean mixtures from the chippy and you may be wondering what they are. You took a basin to the chippy, any size, and peas or beans were put in first and followed by chips, then pea or beans soup poured over it if you wished. Depending on the size of your bowl it might cost threepence or sixpence. So, you see it would be a cheap meal to have in the middle of the week when funds were getting low.

No doubt in certain circumstances a threepence basinful would do two people.

Another Northern speciality is the rag puddings. These were made with suet pastry but instead of lining a basin the pastry is rolled into an oblong – the meat and onions are then placed in the centre, seasoned and the pastry brought up to the centre, overlapped, and the edges all turned over to look like an envelope. It is then wrapped in a pudding cloth which can be anything made from white cotton or muslin, and pinned together and then dropped into a pan of boiling water and boiled for at least two hours. The water must be kept boiling at all times. If it starts to dry up, only boiling water must be added to it.

The chip shops used to sell these puddings and women also used to make them for their families. If it was for one of the menfolk the puddings would be so big, they would be hanging off the sides of the plate. Nothing else was needed to eat with it, as it would be filling on its own.

Once again, the advent of rationing put a stop to all of this. From coming to Bournemouth from Oldham we had not had a decent meat pudding. Then one year we went up there to see Norman. We were looking for a chippy to get something for supper. When we found one, we saw the notice in the window 'rag puddings sold here'. We couldn't wait to get inside and buy two and they were just a delicious as we remembered them. We also found a stall in the market which sold them to take away. We asked if they would freeze and the stall holder said yes, so we bought six and cooked one a week! I have a go at making one sometimes but for some reason they never turn out right.

During the evenings men would come around selling hot potatoes - very small ones. They were lovely. Also, black peas, another tasty dish. All these things seemed to have disappeared from the face of the earth. The seller would call out 'hot potatoes! Come and get your hot potatoes". I loved the black peas. There again you went with a basin and asked for three pence and sixpence worth, with plenty of soup. One ate them with a slice of bread and put plenty vinegar of them. I find them delicious but I have never seen any here in the South. The hot potatoes were also sold on the fairground.

The other Northern special I remember is wimberry tarts and cream. There again there aren't many places one can buy wimberry tarts, only confectionery shops. But one could buy wimberry itself to make one's own wimberry tarts. It was usually in season in August and early September and it was easy to tell who had had wimberry pie for their dinner as it had a tendency to turn your mouth and lips blue, but who cared? It was so good.

I shall have to stop writing about all this food, it's making me drool with longing for these dishes of yesteryear. They still make wimberry tarts in the shops in Oldham. We bought some last time we were up there when we went to Melia's funeral but couldn't find any wimberry in the fruiterers shops.

Tripe is also very popular in the North, and black puddings. The only tripe I like is honeycombe which looks exactly like its name suggests. On hot days it is ideal raw with lots of vinegar on it, and a slice of bread and butter. I used to have it quite a lot when I worked in the mill and it was hot.

More Schooldays

Back to my schooldays - After Miss Sanderson's class came Standard Two. Miss Tanner's class. There we learned to do some knitting, chain stitch, embroidery, raffia work, darning and plain sewing. In addition to learning some geography, we had sums, reading etc. with Miss Simpson who was known to be a bit of a terror and was ever ready to use the cane on those who would not learn or misbehaved,

During the time we were in Standard Two, Empire Day came along. This happened once a year and all the schools dressed up to represent a country of the British Empire. Our school, St Marks, was Ceylon, which is now Sri Lanka. All the girls were dressed in saris. We were allowed to choose between two colours, brown or green. I think I chose green and then we had our faces browned with gravy browning to look Indian. On the day itself all the schools in Chadderton took part in a parade and people came to watch us go by. One girl, Marian Batey was chosen to be a princess and got to ride in style, but I can't remember what was used for a carriage. At the end of the parade the schools all finished up at North Chadderton School and were given refreshments before being picked up by their parents. The boys of St Luke's school were all in sailor suits, representing Malta, a place I had never heard of at the time. In Miss Tanner's class we learned to do joined up writing or real writing as it was usually called. Mr Rogers was the headmaster but he also took standard four which was the last class before moving to North

Chadderton senior school. I was looking forward to going there because in the last year one got the opportunity to go on a day out in London and as no-one in our family had ever been there, I couldn't wait to be the first to go. I was really looking forward to my final term and the trip to see all the places we had learned about - the Tower of London, Houses of Parliament, Westminster Abbey, Big Ben, the cenotaph, all these things I found fascinating. I had always been interested in history lessons, and history and geography were my two favourite subjects. St Marks had reckoned without Hitler of course. Because of the war all trips were off as you would imagine they would be, with all the bombing and all that. So, I was done out of my chance to see what London was like. It was several years after leaving school before I actually got to going there. Six years later I believe.

Mr Rogers being the headmaster as well as taking class was quite a busy man. So sometimes he would give me the responsibility of marking the sums done by the rest of the class. Any I found correct I had to check how it had been worked out and not and make sure they were right and that no-one had just put in a correct answer they had copied. Any I was not sure of I handed over to Mr Rogers to check himself. One boy in the class - Walter Sparrow - was hopeless – never got anything right. In fact he never did anything. Whatever we had to do we always had to put our name at the top of the page. That was as far as Walter ever got. The rest of the time would be spent sucking the end of his pen. He couldn't even get his name right. He always got the S of Sparrow round the wrong way. I expect that anyone like that these days would be in a special needs class but no-one seemed to care about anyone who was like Walter.

When we got to North Chad (that's what we called it for short) our class from St Marks was split up. Some of us went into an A class and some of us into a B. We were joined by pupils from other schools. After a week or two we were all given an intelligence test to ascertain if we were in the correct division. What I didn't like about North Chad was the way the teachers were always pushing you to play sports. I didn't like running or any games that involved running which meant most of them. I was not a physical person at all. Also, I didn't like getting into the swimming baths. I hated water and getting wet. I believe I am still the same now. We used to go every Monday morning at eleven-thirty and when we came out at noon we could then go straight home. At that time, although now living at home, I still had my dinners at my Grandma's and as she lived just round the corner from the baths I was soon indoors and drying off. When we had games, Miss Hilton, the sports mistress would choose two girls to be captains and they were allowed to choose their own teams. This was for netball and hockey. I was always the last to be chosen. I didn't blame them. I knew I was hopeless. However, when on the other hand teams were chosen for a quiz, I was then the first. So, I shone in some respect. We can't all be good at the same things. In all the three years I was at North Chad I never learned to swim and I still can't.

We never had a school uniform - just wore navy blue gymslips with a white blouse underneath – short sleeve in summer and long sleeve in winter. I think it was due to the clothing coupons that we didn't have to have a uniform. We didn't get many coupons and they were needed for other clothing. Some school wear was off coupons for example navy blue knickers which is what we all wore. Whenever we had games or sports, we removed our gymslips and tucked everything else in our knickers. This also happened when we were outside. Unfortunately, this brought a few 'dirty old men' as we used to call them to stand outside the school playground railings and gaze at us showing off our legs. Our headmistress Miss Stansfield was always coming out to order them away but they came back again as soon as she disappeared. In the end we just had to ignore them. North Chad boys school was part of the same building as the girls but fortunately for us they had their playtime an sports at different times to us otherwise we would have had them staring at us goggle eyed as well.

My favourite subject at North Chad was always maths closely followed by history, geography and English literature and English. In English we usually had to do an essay and we were marked in composition, punctuation and spelling etc and neatness and handwriting. The marks for each of these were a maximum of ten out of ten, thirty out of thirty in total. I usually managed to get anything from twenty-five to twenty-eight. I found history fascinating and could never get enough of learning about places like Stonehenge, the bronze age, the stone age, etc kings and queens of the past, people who were sent to the tower, people who were executed and many more historical aspects. Mrs Phinn was the one that took us for geography and she had a very hands-on approach. When the Japanese bombed Pearl Harbour in the South Pacific she started to teach us about the Polynesian Islands and Hawaii in particular. She showed us how to do the hula hula and had us all out in front of the class dancing away. The only trouble was we had no music to dance to so it rather spoiled it as we were all dancing to a different time, some slow, some fast, Another day she had us learning Morris dancing but we much preferred the hula hula.

Miss Cheetham was our history teacher and in addition to history she also taught us about government and how the country is run with cabinet ministers etc and the office of the chancellor of the exchequer and how he gets his money in to run the country. She also took us on nature rambles and taught us the names of lots of wild plants and flowers and how to recognise them. She also showed us how to recognise trees by the shape of their leaves. I can still remember some of them but not all. When we were doing politics we were shown how elections were run. Two candidates would be put up, although no party politics would be mentioned, but each candidate would have to state what they represented and the rest of the class would vote for one or other depending on opinion. We had boxes to represent a ballot box, and voting slips, so it was all very realistic.

Miss Holmes took us for domestic science which covered cooking, washing, ironing, cleaning. All of us did cooking every week but the other jobs we took in turn. Whatever we cooked we were allowed to take home but sometimes we cooked something for the staff room for those teachers that did not go home for lunch. I hope they enjoyed it – we never had any complaints.

The headmistress, Miss Stansfield, took us for music. The songs we sung were such as 'Who is Sylvia?' 'Nymphs and Shepherds'. Sweet lass of Richmond Hill," and many others and Miss Hilton took us for dancing. That would be country dancing of course which is very similar to morris dancing. We asked her if we could learn ballroom dancing instead. She agreed providing we provided the records for the music, which we agreed to do. We paid a penny a week from all of us. Each week we raised about two shillings and nine pence. Records were about two shillings and six pence. We chose the records. Sometimes Miss Hilton was happy with our choice and sometimes she was not. There was a dance orchestra around at that time by the name of Victor Sylvester and his strict tempo orchestra. When we bought something like this, she was happy but when we bought "In The Mood" or 'American Patrol' she was most disapproving but we didn't let it stop us.

One day we, that is our class, Form 4, were in trouble over something or other, can't remember what it was now, but as a punishment Miss Hilton decided our dance class should be handed over to Form 3 and we would have to take another subject. She also intended that they should use our records. This did not go down too well with us at all. We tried to remonstrate with her but to no avail so we had a little pow-wow between us and came up with the idea that we would go on strike and refuse to take ourselves off to the class she wanted us to attend. We all sat in a ring in the hall, on the floor. Miss Hilton tried one more time to get us to move but we were adamant if she let Form 3 use our records, paid for by us, we were not moving.

At this point she went to bring Miss Stansfield into the situation. I wish I could say that we won in the end but it was not so. The conclusion was that Form 3 were not allowed to use our records but we, Form 4 were banned from our dancing classes for one month so I don't know who was the winner in that situation.

On another occasion when the whole class had to be punished again it was Miss Stansfield who decided the punishment. After giving us all the strap on our hands – one stroke each, she sent the whole class to an extra two-hour math class at the end of the week. Then she turned to me and said 'that doesn't apply to you. You will do two hours needlework instead.' Obviously, she knew how I felt about needlework and that sentencing me to two hours math would have been a pleasure not a punishment.

Blackpool

As I have already stated previously, the Rayners and our family always went to Blackpool every year for our holidays. I think I must have been accident prone because one year Eileen and I were holding hands in Stanley Park and running towards one of the lily ponds. When we got to the edge Eileen had the good sense to let go of my hand and step back from the edge. I on the other hand kept on running and went slap straight into the pond. It was a horrible feeling. I really thought I was drowning. I managed to claw my way out. I was absolutely soaked of course and we all had to make our way back to the boarding house so that I could dry off. I was very upset and cried all the way back. Stanley Park was quite a way from central Blackpool where we were staying. It was too far to walk and we had to use the bus. Everyone seemed to be staring at me with all my clothes dripping wet. I was never so glad to see the boarding house. Another year I fell down the stairs from top to bottom and yet I never hurt myself. My mother expected me to have broken bones but no, I got over that alright. I always seemed to have one disaster or another but the one that upset us all the most was when I went down with measles two days before we were due to travel. My dad had to phone the boarding house to cancel. No-one bothered with insurance in those days so he lost both his deposit and also the remainder of the cost of the holiday.

When we went to Blackpool the cheapest way to have a holiday was by staying in apartments. This was what most people did. You bought your own food and were given a cupboard or half a cupboard in the dining room in which to keep this food. Meat and fish you bought fresh every day and gave it to the landlady. She was the one who did all the cooking - whatever you brought in she would cook it for you. Sweets and dessert she would make up herself and provide at a small cost. For these privileges you would be charged an amount to include the room, hot water, (in a jug and basin) cooking, desserts, etc and another one shilling and sixpence for the cruet. Full board was available to those that could afford it which wasn't very many at that time but after the war finished it was full board for almost everyone. Apartments were no longer a paying proposition for landladies. Most boarding houses would provide full board for between four pounds and five pounds per person per week. Obviously, the apartments were much cheaper – about two pounds per person per week – without the food - the cost of which was up to yourself. Whether or not you enjoyed the landladies cooking was another matter but if it was not to your liking then you wouldn't go there again.

Eileen and I had our favourite part of Blackpool and that was the Pleasure Beach – an enormous fairground. I believe at that time it was the largest in Europe and the only fairground larger was Coney Island in New York. We loved the Pleasure Beach and fortunately for us so did my Dad. Eileen's parents weren't so keen to go on any of the rides, nor was my mother, although there were a couple she would go on. Some of the rides me and Eileen were allowed to go on by ourselves but some of them like the Big Dipper my dad went on with me. By today's standards they now seem a bit tame but in those days they were the bees knees. The other thing my Dad liked about the pleasure beach were the stalls where one could try your luck to win a prize or two. My dad had one in particular he enjoyed. One rolled a ball into some holes and depending on the number of the hole a monkey would climb up a stick. The first person to reach the top of the stick would be the winner and be able to choose a prize. Albert played the game also but he wasn't as good as my dad who had it off to a fine art.

We always went to the shows in Blackpool. They were well-known for being the best shows in the country. All the famous stars were there plus the Tower Circus - that was always worth going to. My dad used to book a different show every night. South Pier, Central Pier, North Pier, Operahouse, Winter Gardens, and Tower Circus. These were always evening shows naturally so we always had somewhere go all day. I never enjoyed the beach but Eileen did with her bucket and spade. I used to moan and sulk when I had to give way and play on the sands but I did like the donkey rides.

Whitsun

Another Northern custom took place around Whitsuntide. This time was about seven weeks after Easter and mostly involved the churches – especially the Catholic church. The children who would be all dressed up in white, girls in dresses with white socks and shoes and boys in white shirts and navy shorts and blazers would be lined up and starting from the church they normally attended they would then walk through the town. Those who belonged to an organisation like the girl guides or the brownies or in the case of the boys, the boys brigade, or scouts, or sea cadets, would wear the normal uniform. The Catholic were always the best attended because their churches were always the best attended, more so than the Church of England turn out. The little girls also carried small baskets of flowers, or posies, and some of the kiddies were very young, but there were always grown-ups to help them out. There were two days when these walks took place – one was Whit Friday and the other was Whit Sunday. Some churches walked on the Friday and some on the Sunday. It was generally known as 'walking round.' Lots of people lined the streets to watch all the different churches go by.

Whitsunday was also the day for wearing your new clothes. Those who could afford it would kit out their children in all new clothes which they would have been buying for several weeks leading up to Whitsun. Some would have all new from top to bottom, girls - vest, knickers, underslip, dress, coat and hat, socks and shoes. Boys had underwear, shirt, pants (trousers) (short or long depending on age), socks and shoes, jackets or blazers. You got up on Whitsunday morning and after breakfast got dressed in your new outfit. Then depending on age, you would either be taken by your mother to visit as many of your relatives as lived close enough by. or you might be expected to go yourself, to show off your new clothes. You always got money for this visit. Sometimes only coppers - two or three pence but if it was close relatives it would be more like sixpence. You also went into the next door neighbours' house. As well as you yourself going around to visit certain people there would also be some people coming to your own house for which your parents would be paying out money here and there. I never found out where this custom came from originally. All I can think of is because Oldham was a Lancashire mill town it was to persuade parents to buy goods and keep the mills running but I never heard of it in any other Lancashire town - just Oldham. Not everyone was able to spend all that money on new clothes for their children every year. Those with large families for instance might buy clothes for just one of their children each year or even not at all. Being an only child, I was lucky enough to be able to have 'new clothes' every year - as my father was forever telling me.

I would like to point out that this business of 'new clothes' came to a stop when a child had become a worker unless he or she wanted to pay for them themselves. I have often wondered when the tradition eventually died out. I know it was still going strong in 1963. I was buying clothes for you at that time and then we moved to Bournemouth in 1969 so I cannot say for sure when it died out.

My friends Elsie and Violet

When I was around nine years old Elsie Harrison came to live in Park View. She had previously been living, along with her parents, at her grandmother's home that was on a farm quite a way down Broadway and at last the council had given them a house on the Park estate. Although I was still living at my grandma's address during the week at the weekend I would be at home and so got quite friendly with Elsie and I started to go to the farm with her on Sundays and have tea there. There wasn't much in the way of animals there, one horse called Veleta, one cow they kept for milk, a few hens, ducks, etc and that was it. We had lots of space to play and when the weather was wet and cold, we had two swings to play on in the barn under cover, which had been fixed up by her grandad. There was no running water in the house – the water came from a well.

The back of the farm backed onto a cricket field and if there were no matches being played, we used to have races round the field. When the war started in 1939 the Ministry of Defence wanted horses for the battlefield and they came to take Veleta away. I believe we all cried a little on that day. They promised to bring her back when the war finished but none of us ever saw her again, nor did we ever find out what happened to her.

Like me, Elsie was having piano lessons but as she was eighteen months older than me, she had been going longer and so was much further advanced. There was no piano at the farm but they did have an organ that Elsie could also play. I used to try and play but I could never get my feet to move in conjunction with my hands. It was not a modern organ as you would expect to see nowadays – more like a church organ. Elsie's Dad could play both the organ and the piano but he could not read music. He played 'by ear' as it was termed. Once he had heard a piece of music, he could usually play it afterwards. He had an evening job at a pub playing the piano. His 'piece de resistance' was "The Warsaw Concerto'. This came from a film all about the Invasion of Poland by the Nazis in 1940. The film was called 'Dangerous Moonlight' and the music was written especially for the film. It was sort of semi-classical and everyone enjoyed listening to it. And Jimmy Harrison (Elsie's dad) always tried to make it the last piece of the evening. And it usually brought the house down. I had the music for it and it was not an easy piece to play. It took a lot of practice to master it, but I persevered until I got it right.

I very soon got another friend in addition to Elsie. A girl called Violet Moore and her family came to live in Park Avenue very close to where I was. She was older than both Elsie and myself. Elsie was now ready to leave school at fourteen but I had another twelve months to go before I left. Violet had already left school and was going out to work. She was working where her father worked at the C.W.S jam factory preparing the fruit for the jam. Sometimes she would be working on the pickle side of the factory and not the jam and on these occasions one could smell the vinegar on her clothes. Elsie's first job was at Meredith and Drew's biscuit factory but that didn't last long. She didn't like the hours. It was shift work six am to two pm one week and two pm to ten pm the following week. I can't say I blame her for leaving that job behind although to give her her due she did stick it out for six months before packing in. Her next job was in the cardroom at the Elk Mill. It was hard work but the hours were better –seven-thirty pm to five-thirty pm, five days per week. The Elk was a very up to date mill having showers for the women in the card room and showers for the men in the spinning room. Not many of the mills at that time could boast that. There was also one of the best canteens around and lorry drivers would always try to finish near the Elk at lunchtime as it had very good cooks.

The three of us, Elsie, Violet and myself, started to go out together to the pictures. The picture houses were The Luric, The Casino and The Imperial. The Casino was allowed to open on Sundays when war started. Occasionally we would go into Oldham to the Odeon or the Gaumont. We had six different cinemas in Oldham at that time. In addition to the Odeon and The Gaumont there was also the Palladium which we christened the iceberg because it was always so cold in there. Then there was the Grosvenor which was lovely and elegant, The Kings' which also had a cafe and The Victory which was the cheapest of the lot both in looks and in price. Saturday nights we sometimes went dancing instead of the cinema, at Kings' Street Stores or wherever we could get tickets for. There were two places as well where one could learn dancing, downstairs for the learners and upstairs for those who could dance already. The other place one could go to learn to dance was Eddie Cooke's, where one danced to records.

To go to the cinema in those days one had to be prepared to queue for ages and that didn't have to be any special film. It was for every film, every night. There were four different prices one shilling and sixpence, one shilling and ninepence, two shillings and three pence, and two shillings and ninepence. The most popular seats were the one and nine's. They were reasonably priced and had the best position in the cinema. Blokes who wanted to take out a girl were expected to pay for her and the one and nines they could usually afford (once a week anyway). I expect these prices will seem quite cheap compared to today. Dancing was a little bit more expensive than the cinema and girls usually paid for themselves for dancing – around two shillings and six pence depending on who the band was. We didn't normally bother with those.

Close to the farm lived a doctor and his wife, Dr and Mrs Wells. They had two children who were older than Elsie and myself and were both at university. Leslie and Margaret were their names and we only saw them at holiday times. Christmas time was the best. Elsie's grandma would put on a big spread and the Wells' family would be there along with Elsie's parents, younger sisters, and myself, plus of course the grandad. And Mrs Harrison's brother uncle Sam. Mrs Harrison always made her own ice cream and it was delicious - better than anything you could buy in the shops. When we had all eaten Leslie and Margaret would do the washing up and then they would organise party games in which we all joined in. I think I went three times to one of those parties. It was always too late for me to go back home when the evening was over so I slept over, as did Elsie's sisters, and then we all went home the following morning. These were some of the best Christmases I had as a child.

We had sing-songs as well with Elsie and her dad on the piano and the organ. Very musical evenings. I was learning to play the piano myself at this time and sometimes I was able to join in with what they were playing. After two years my piano teacher decided to retire and he recommended another tutor – a woman - not very far away. I did not like her very much. If I played a wrong note, she tapped me on the knuckles with a ruler and sometime it was harder than others. After twelve months of being with her I decided to pack it in just before I was taking my first exam. Looking back, I wish I had taken that exam. If I had passed, I might have gone on to better things but there we are. It was not to be. And so my musical education came to an abrupt end. I still carried on playing of course. Every Saturday afternoon my dad gave me some money to buy some music from a stall in Oldham market. Sometimes I could play the music almost immediately others I needed to practice for days but I was always on the piano. No-one needed to tell me to practise. At the time we had a dog called Vic and whenever he heard the piano he would come and sit by the side of it and even if he was outside if he heard it he would come in and sit by my side. So at least I knew someone appreciated my efforts. Mind you I don't know what Jacksons next door thought of it although as far as I know they never complained so perhaps they enjoyed it. I bought all sorts of music – popular songs of the day, plus some semi-classical stuff - Chopin, Liszt, Schubert, Ravel, Tchaikovsky, Strauss and lots of others.

Bonfires and Maypoles

In the 1930's before the onset of the second world war, there were lots of large bonfires around for Guy Fawkes night. Sometimes families would combine and have one very big bonfire. The women would make treacle toffee – trays and trays of it. They also provided potatoes for baking in the bonfire. Mostly the bonfires would be held on waste ground and all who had collected the wood for it or provided anything else were very welcome to attend. These large bonfires lit up the area for miles around so when the war began large bonfires were banned. One could still have small ones as these would not be seen from the

German planes flying overhead, but they were not as exciting. The wood for the bonfire whether large or small was collected up by the kids. They would start weeks before November fifth and start to build it up in a suitable place where there was little risk. All the kids in the neighbourhood would be employed in this activity and on occasions when one lot found someone else had a larger stack than themselves, they would raid it, that is to say carry away as much wood as they could. This went on all during the weeks prior to the big night. First one lot would have the bigger pile of wood, then it would be another and so it went on. The wood itself was collected from anywhere you found it hanging about but it was always wood that no-one wanted.

On the big night itself, one of the men would take it upon himself to light the bonfire. When it was deemed hot enough the potatoes would go in. They needed a lot of cooking and a very hot fire. The outside skins used to be black and hard but inside they were lovely. When you got them out of the fire, they were so hot you had to juggle them from one hand to another. Also, the treacle toffee would be passed around but this was cooked indoors not on the fire. If anyone had made a guy it would be thrown on the fire towards the end of proceedings to give the fire a boost. We had fireworks as well and got the money for the fireworks from cob-coaling. We went from house to house singing a special cob-coaling song the words of which went as follows:

'We come a cob-coaling
For bonfire time,
Your coal and your money we hope you enjoy
For down in yon cellar, there's an old um-ber-ella
And nowt on yon Cornish but an old pepper pot
Pepper pot, pepper pot, morning till night
If you give'd us nowt, we'll steal nowt and bid you good night
Christmas Is coming

The geese are getting fat
Please put a penny in the old man's hat
If you haven't got a penny a ha'penny will do
If you haven't got a ha'penny then God bless you
Up a ladder, down a wall
A cob o coal 'll save us all'

It doesn't make much sense I know, but it sounds better when you hear it sung, especially by a chorus of kids

When we had finished singing, we would knock on the door and ask "Please can you help our bonfire."

Most people were willing to give us a few coppers. I enjoyed cob-coalling much more than Christmas Day.

Nowadays more people attend community bonfires which is a good thing in my view. I believe cob-coalling has gone out of fashion. One more tradition from my childhood gone.

'I skip the May-pole, the May-pole, the May-pole
I skip the May-pole, Tra -la-la-la-la- la'

The first of May brought out the little girls with their maypoles. These were made up of two hoops. Usually procured from a shop which had butter or something similar delivered in a barrel with two hoops around. First the hoops would be wrapped in coloured tissue paper and then placed one within the other in a crosswise direction. These hoops would then be nailed on top of a broom handle which had also been wrapped around with coloured paper and several paper ribbons attached to this depending on how many maypole dancers there were. Usually it was around four or five. There would also be a May Queen, a young child of tender years fulfilling this role and sitting at the bottom of the pole on a tuffet (small stool). Elsie and I always had her younger sister Ivy, for May Queen. Whilst all the dancing round the Maypole was taking place, there would be at least one person knocking and asking for a penny or so. 'Please will you help our maypole' is what we usually said. We never stayed in the same street for long. Perhaps do two set ups, and then move on to the next street. What was annoying was to turn the corner of one street and find someone else had set up in the same street you wanted to dance in.., or when you yourself had set up to dance and someone else came along to disrupt. People didn't like being asked to 'help our maypole' twice. When we decided we had had enough and there was no more money forthcoming we would pack up and go home. We had been in our best dresses for the maypole so now we could change back into our playing out clothes and dismantle the maypole. We would also count the pennies we had collected and share it between us. And that would be that until the next May.

We were able to set up in the middle of the street because there was no traffic. There must have been lots of maypoles in my grandmothers' day. From what I have been told, whole communities had them on the village greens. Sometimes there would be a May fair at the same time. But you have to remember days like May Day where their only holiday. May Day in the nineteenth century must have been quite exciting especially for the younger ones. You never knew who you might meet at the fair. In later years, after the war, and more cars came to be on the roads, maypoles died out. It was too dangerous. So that was another era at an end – no more children's maypoles.

Teenage Years

As I got older, I discovered two things. One was 'boys' and one was 'The Green'. I don't think I need to go into any revelations about the discovery of boys, practically every girl knows how that comes about, but as far as 'The Green' is concerned it may require some explanation. As I have mentioned before in The Jones chapter, "The Green' was in the centre of Oldham and was used as part of the market. and also for when the fairground came to town. Oldham wakes was a very large fair and some of it had to be spun off on to the green. When the war came there were three rides still on there but they were unable to move for several reasons, one being shortage of fuel for their enormously large wagons which moved their machines from one place to another. Also, as every showman was in the same boat there wasn't really anywhere for them to go. So, they were stuck here in Oldham and if they wanted to remain open and continue making money they had two choices – open daytime only, which wasn't financially viable or black out everything so that not a chink of light was showing through and so they could then open in the evenings. And this is what they did. Violet Moores had a friend, Joyce Lord, who worked at the Jam works and used to go on the green and persuaded Vi to come up one night. She in turn asked me if I would like to go with her. As I was always fond of fairs I agreed and that was the start of my 'green' days. When one approached the tent it all was pitch black and then as one entered through the flap it was like another world all bright lights and loud music and lots of people and noise. I absolutely loved it. Violet and I went every Friday and Saturday night and yes we met boys there too, The rides were never more than tuppence each except for the last one of the night when the price went up to threepence but you got a longer ride. My favourite was the steamboats. We always stood up at the back. The steamboat went up and down and you travelled higher on the upward movement and coming down again gave you a bigger thrill. Our green days lasted two years and then the war came to an end and everyone moved on and the council took over the land and built a Littlewoods Store there. All the caravans that people were still living in had to be moved. I don't know where they all went but I think the council found houses for them. I know there weren't that many by that time. One family I got to know quite well were the Holdens'. They had a small kiddie's roundabout on Tommyfield. That was the name of the large market ground and they were in operation every Monday, Friday and Saturday. Those were the market days. I don't know how they did financially but I think they did alright. There was always a queue for it.

I got to know Tilly Holden first through going to Billington's dancing. She had noticed me on the green and one night came over to me and we started to talk. Also about this time the steamboats moved off and a family called Ingham arrived in their place. They brought with them a set of dodgems. They also had a son Billy who was very good looking and after I had been going up to the dodgems for about three to four weeks, he asked me out. He also asked if Elsie who was with me at the time would come as well for George who was Tilly's brother. She agreed but later gave up going with him but Billy and myself carried on. He used to meet me off the number six bus in Oldham which used to stop close to the green about five-thirty, and then we would go to the cinema first, and then another one when we came out of the first one. Billy always paid to go in the dearest seats in the circle and bought us ice cream or chocolate. Sometimes if George did not have enough money Billy would pay for all four of us.

His only job was working on the dodgems so his dad must have paid him well. However, all good things must come to an end someday and the Inghams and the dodgems moved on. I believe they went to Northenden in Cheshire. I never saw him again after that. When Oldham Wakes was on and there were dodgems there, I would look to see whose name was on them but never saw 'Ingham' up there. When we were kids 'Oldham Wakes' was one of the most exciting times of the year and I don't just mean the fair itself. It was the arrival that made it so exciting. Coming up Middleton Road with those enormous diesel lorries, all packed with the different rides and roundabouts. They each had their own plot on the market ground and they would start to unpack almost immediately. There was always loads of kids watching because we knew once it was up and running, they would let us climb aboard and get free rides. This was always on a Thursday afternoon and Thursday night onwards it was pay time. The wakes would be on Friday, Saturday and Monday and by Tuesday they had started to dismantle the rides ready to move on to the next port of call. Oldham Wakes was always at the end of August and all the cotton factories closed down for a week and those who wanted to go on holiday (and could afford to) would take their annual week's leave, usually to Blackpool, as we and the Rayners did.

We, that is my mother and father and myself, would usually go on the 'wakes' on a Friday night before going off to Blackpool on Saturday morning. So, this Friday night was also very exciting as there was the coming holiday to look forward to as well as the night on the 'wakes'. I always hoped my dad would decide to stay until darkness fell because I liked to see it all lit up, bright lights, and lots of noise and music. The old fairground organs were the best, like they have at these steam rallies. The war spoiled a lot of it though – the blackout ruined the night time, the people who ran the rides had to keep everything undercover and it wasn't the same. Well I think that's enough about Oldham Wakes and I have written about my holidays in Blackpool and how accident prone I was so we will move on to the days when I left school at fourteen.

V.E. Day

Everyone was aware in May that the war was almost at an end, and when on the sixth May it was announced on the radio that the following day would be Victory in Europe day and a public holiday. In fact there were two days of public holidays. As you can imagine everyone was cock-a-hoop. It was suggested by the Government that we have street parties and generally celebrate the ending of hostilities. Bonfires were now to be permitted and the ringing of church bells which during the war were only to be rung to signify an invasion. People started to club together towards street parties and bunting to decorate the streets. Some people, like my father, took the fairy lights which were normally only used at Christmas and put them outside in the shape of V. It was decided amongst the residents of our street that we would hire a marquee in case it should rain, but it didn't. The weather was perfect. Trestle tables were set up, and our piano was commandeered for the music. Jimmy Harrison, Elsie's father, was elected to play it (actually he was the only one who could play it). The night before the proceedings he came to our house for a practice and we couldn't get him off it. He sat there playing for hours. He just wouldn't go home. I think he went all through his repertoire. He didn't play from music - just by ear.

My mother wasn't too pleased though because with the marquee being opposite our back gate everyone who wanted to use the toilet nipped through our back garden, in the back door, and up to the toilet. Finally, she got so fed up with it she locked the back door, which was a nuisance for ourselves but necessary otherwise they would have been going up the stairs in their droves. We had lots of lovely food. I don't know where it all came from considering we had been rationed for the last five years but everyone mucked in and put on a good spread. It turned out to be a very enjoyable night.

The following day was V.E day plus one. Our gang, which comprised me, Elsie, Billy Wood, Johnny Beaver, George Horsfield and Joe Shepherd (whom I couldn't stand!) went everywhere together. We heard there was to be dancing at Chadderton Town Hall and we decided to there. There were fireworks as well and we spotted many bonfires on our way to the town hall. There were many people there and we all had a great time. I think I enjoyed it even more because Johnny and I had been estranged for two weeks (due to Elsie's interference) but on that night we got back together (it didn't last long though and we were soon split up again!). Unfortunately, it was back to work the next day.

Going to the pictures to see war films was exciting after V.E day knowing that what was being shown was no longer happening. However, what was shown on the newsreels was the liberation of the concentration camps like Belsen and Auschwitz.

We didn't know anything about these camps until they were shown on the newsreels and they came as a shock to everyone who saw them. To see the state of the prisoners was shocking to us. Whenever those pictures were shown the whole cinema would go quiet like a deathly hush had fallen on the place. These prisoners were just skin and bone when the allied troops found them. Those newsreels were shown for weeks until the prisoners were finally all released. I believe that was just about the worst time of the war, to think that these camps had been in existence during the whole of the war and we knew nothing about them. However, life went on here in England and soon it was time for a General Election to be called. There was nothing else on people's lips that summer but the election. Winston Churchill was the leader of the Conservative party and as he had been such a popular and strong Prime Minister throughout the war quite a few people expected him to lead the Tories to victory, but it didn't happen. Instead the Labour party, led by Clement Attlee, had a landslide victory. The country had had many conservative governments in the past who had done nothing for the working classes. This time the working classes were determined that they would be in charge of their own destiny. Lots of things changed for the better after this: shorter working hours, free prescriptions, free eye and dental practices. This was the start of the NHS. In 1948 everyone paid a sum of money into the system to cover all expenses including children's expenses and hospital treatment for the whole family. It's a far cry from those days to now.

Also, there was a free allowance of tobacco or cigarettes for pensioners. Unemployment benefit was increased as was sick benefit. So, all in all it was a good period. Of course, like all good things it had to come to an end and a few years later the Labour party were beaten decisively and the conservatives were in again. It wasn't until the sixties, and Harold Wilson that we had another Labour government.

Nora the Young Woman

First Job

When we had the Christmas holidays, those whose fourteenth birthday fell during that two-week period and before the date of returning to school were allowed to leave school and look for a job. However, if like me your birthday fell after the date for returning to school you had to carry on until the end of the next term. So much to my disgust I had to carry on until Easter. The teachers did not know what to do with me as I had already been through the curriculum and I was already a prefect and Vice head of School. Miss Kershaw, who was the maths teacher, decided to give me lessons in Algebra. It was something new, a challenge, but there again, when it came time for me to leave, I had to cut it out, which was a pity.

The Elk Mill applied to the school for a 'suitable girl' to work in their office – conversant with figures, English and good handwriting. Miss Stansfield recommended me and I subsequently went for an interview and a little test to see if my spelling and punctuation were suitable, and also if I was any good with figures. I must have passed on all counts because I got the job. And so that was the beginning of my relationship with the Elk Mill, which lasted for three years altogether although I wasn't doing the same job all the time.

There were two more girls in the office – Alma Taylor, whom I had never met before, and Irene Bowker, whom I had known from North Chad although she was at least two years older than me. They were quite helpful in the first couple of months until I got to learn the ropes and then I could manage on my own and understood what was needed.

There were also two men in the office – Henry Gartside - whom we called Mr. Henry – also Mr Massey who was the sales rep. He went down once a week to the Cotton Exchange to buy raw cotton for the mill to keep the mill running. Another part of his job was to get orders for the mill. We hardly ever saw Mr Massey except when he got back from his travels around five pm. He never came into the office in the mornings.

There was also a manager, Mr Graver, but he had his own office. He was more to do with the day to day running of the mill. He was a very cheerful soul. Always whistling.

I think I should have mentioned another of the requisites the firm wanted from me was typing. I had already been attending a shorthand and typing school so I was able to type well enough for their requirements.

Fortunately, they didn't need any shorthand as I didn't quite get on with that somehow. It is very complicated. The shorthand alphabet being phonetic each sound being represented by a symbol, for example, / would represent p as in plum. Vowels were dots and dashes and depending on where they were on the line, above on or below would indicate which vowel they were representing. I did not get past the first few lessons. But I enjoyed the typing. Looking back to the typewriters we were taught on they look so outdated compared to today's standards. But it is only the machines that have changed – the keyboard and typing is just the same.

It was at The Elk Mill that I first came into contact with my first husband. That was Leslie Smith. But I had no desire to get to know him at that time. In fact, there was another lad, Jack Baynham, in whom I was more interested at the time. Les often asked me out but I always said no, whereas when Jack asked me out, I said yes. My duties in the office at that time were typing invoices, sending out letters, answering the phone, making up wages, doing the National Insurance stamps, working out the PAYE, making morning coffee and afternoon tea. After I had been there twelve months it was decided to have a yarn tester and I was offered the job. This was to be a full-time job so another girl had to be employed to do the work that I had been doing up until then, so enter Margaret Taylor. Margaret was quite a girl. She was very good looking, had bags of personality, was witty and generally well-liked by everyone, particularly members of the opposite sex. She was only fourteen but had a fantastic figure and had everyone of the male species falling over themselves to arrange a date with her. Yet for all that, even the girls couldn't help liking her. She could lure your boyfriend away, anyone's boyfriend, and no-one became upset about it and she was never hated for it. We all liked her.

To train for this new job as yarn tester I was sent to a place out at Didsbury which is between Manchester and Cheshire. I had to travel there every day. The firm paid my expenses of course. Bus fares, meals etc. I quite enjoyed it and was sorry when it came to an end and had to go back to the Elk and start to do the job I had been trained for! The place I went to was called The Shirley Institute and had lots of students being taught about the cotton industry. I was there for four weeks and then I was supposed to know it all. I quite liked the new job as it gave me more access to the inside of the mill itself and the cotton operatives. When working in the office I had felt quite aloof from the rest of the workforce (which I suppose I was meant to feel) but now I could associate myself more as I had daily contact with everyone in the card room, the spinning room, and the warehouse. One thing I should point out when I first went to work at the Elk on leaving school, I discovered that Elsie was working there in the card room so that was a bonus for me as I had to go into the card room every day so we were able to chat during my visits.

Nora's cycling days - Bicycle made For Two

When I first left school I went to work at The Elk Mill in the office. Soon after I started work someone suggested a cycling club. They were very popular at that time. There was a national one called the Cyclists Touring Club (CTC) as well as many private ones. The instigators of our club were Harry Hall and his girlfriend Lena, Eddie Buck and his wife Annie both of whom had done a fair bit of cycling in their younger days also joined. They had tandems. There were three other tandems amongst us, Ab Whitney, Billy Wood and George Marsland. In addition, there was Les and myself. Ab Whitney had his wife riding behind him and he fixed up a chain and pedals in the centre of the tandem for his little daughter to ride in and help out with the pedalling. Elsie Harrison was usually on the back of Bill Wood's tandem and Les and I would be on ours. As for George Marsland he would take anyone who had no other bike to ride, so that was six tandems all told.

To begin with there were not many members but as time went by and new boys and girls came to work at the Elk, the numbers increased. When the club first started, I wasn't too keen. I didn't like the idea of getting up early on Sunday mornings but after a while I had found myself looking forward to Sundays.

Our meeting place was the crossroads of Broadway and Burnley lane. It seemed to be local for most people. It was agreed that nine am on a Sunday morning was to be the departure time. We would have a meeting on the Friday to decide where we were going on the Sunday. We left that up to Harry and Eddie. They had done most of the cycling and knew the best places to visit. It's not just the cycling you go for, but places to stop at cafes and all that - some good - and some not. There was a lot of camaraderie between our own members and members of other clubs when we met up with them in the cafes and other places that were recognised stopping places for cyclists.

All this took place just before the end of the war. The signposts had been removed at the beginning of the war to confuse any paratroopers who might descend from above in the hope of invading the country. In order to find our way about our club relied on Harry Hall and Eddie Buck. They knew their way all over Cheshire, Derbyshire, and the Yorkshire Dales as they had covered them so often in the past.

The first ride we went on was to Hardcastle Crags. I think the name is self-explanatory. It was quite a climb to the top but it was worth it for the view. Coming back down of course was great. Free-wheeling all the way. Our next trip was to Blackstone Edge, an old Roman Road made up of large cobblestones. I believe at one time the stones were to be removed until some heritage realised their importance and history. Next, we went to Lymm in Cheshire. There was a very large cafe there and we had a lot of fun between ourselves there. Lots of laughs. These cafes did not serve food because of rationing. The proprietors would not have had enough food to feed fifteen to twenty people at a time, to be followed by the same number again, so all they were served was tea and we provided our own sandwiches. Due to rationing, dried egg was the favourite, or tomato maybe, but we got by somehow. There was hardly any traffic on the road in those days. If a car did overtake us, they would always laugh and wave, especially if they saw us with a puncture but sometimes the boot was on the other foot when they had broken down and we went shooting past them. Sometimes we went shooting past them even when they weren't in trouble, more so when descending a hill. They needed to engage a lower gear whereas we could just let rip. We always finished at the bottom before them.

The Derbyshire Dales were the best place for uphill and down dale travelling. In the winter, when the snow was covering the hills it was quite a sight. One of the rides I used to love, winter and summer alike, was from Chadderton to Hazel Grove, then Macclesfield to Chapel-en-le-Frith then down Long Hill to Buxton. We parked our bikes in a car park in the centre of Buxton. It cost six pence. We piled our bikes together without any locks – no-one ever thought about locking a bike, a car maybe, but not a bike. As far as I know, no bikes ever got stolen. Certainly, none of ours ever did. Sometimes on Sunday, if no specified ride had been decided, some of us would just cycle around the Cheshire lanes. We were all hoping to come across Reg Harris, who at that time was a champion cyclist, both outdoor and indoor. The best place to come across him was around a village called Chelford, deep in the heart of Cheshire. He tended to hang out at a certain cafe and there were always lots of cyclists hanging out in the same place. The Cheshire lanes were quite flat. Very nice, but too flat for my liking. I liked a bit more variety in my cycling - hard climbs and then some spectacular drop downs, free-wheeling without touching the brakes. It was quite thrilling - as good as a roller coaster ride. When we arrived back at Broadway, we usually went in Bethell's shop for a Dandelion and Burdock or Sarspiralla and oh boy were we ready for it.

One Easter, Les and I, together with George Marsland, Bob Lennox and Maud Whitworth decided we would all go to Llangollen in North Wales for the weekend camping. Maud and I would share a tent and the three lads would also share one. But when we called at Maud's house, she cried off saying she wasn't very well. I don't know if this was true or just an excuse, but either way it made things difficult for me, but Les wanted me to go, so I did. When we arrived in Llangollen, we found a suitable camping place and pitched our tents and then we went down into the town and had something to eat. The cafes were actually the front rooms of all the houses, all complete with genuine welsh dressers with a table in the centre of the room for the customers to sit round. After our beans on toast we had a look round the town. The food and a mug of tea came to one shilling and sixpence each. When we went back to the camp site later there were some other campers there and they had lit a fire. They invited us to join them in sitting around the campfire and they started to sing expecting us to join in with them. At first, we were reluctant but we soon got over our embarrassment and finished up having a good night. I had never sat around a camp fire before, let alone sang round one, so it was something new and quite enjoyable. When we felt it was time to turn in, I made my way to the tent I should have been sharing with Maud but now would be on my own. It had turned cold but fortunately I had borrowed a padded sleeping bag, plus I had brought a couple of blankets, so I wasn't too bad. I don't know if the lads had sleeping bags or just blankets but we all managed to sleep even though it was cold.

    I remember I did the breakfasts that time on a paraffin stove. I also remember I dropped an egg out of the frying pan. As we only had one egg left I scraped it up off the grass and put it back in the pan. The yolk was broken naturally but otherwise no-one knew what had happened it to it so I gave it to George, He never complained so I presumed it was okay. We stayed in Llangollen until after dinner (midday) and then we packed our tents and equipment ready to go home. We set off at four pm expecting to be home by ten pm that evening but unfortunately, we took a wrong turn due to George not reading the map properly and where we should have gone North, we went South instead which put us sixty miles out of our way. We had to traverse quite a few miles to get back on the right track. We were getting so tired we decided we would have to finish our journey by train. By this time, we were near Crewe station (don't ask me how we got there!). We could just about afford the train fare to Manchester. We had to wait two hours for a train and I fell asleep in the waiting room. The music of Glenn Miller was coming over the speaker and helped put me to sleep. That's what I remember most about that night. Whenever I hear Glenn Miller's music played it takes me back to Crewe station. As a consequence of the extra sixty-mile journey my parents were getting worried. When I got home at two am they were very cross. The three lads had already decided they were not going to work the next day, being so tired, but my father made me go in as usual. This didn't go well with the other three as it made them look bad but I didn't blame them. I only wished I could have done the same.

There was one Saturday (a bank holiday weekend) when Elsie and I decided to go to Southport on our bikes a round trip of ninety miles all told. We both felt confident that we could make it and set off in a cheerful mood. We left Chadderton around eight am and arrived in Southport around midday. The first thing to do was to dispose of the bikes. We didn't want to be pushing them round all day. Lots of houses would let you park bikes in their front garden at a cost of six pence for all day. Many of them were already full but we managed to find a garden that still had some space. Once we had disposed of our bikes (and taken note of the house number) we made our way into the town going to the amusements and the funfair. We had brought sandwiches with us in order to cut down on expense so it was decided to eat these right away. We didn't want to carry them round all day. We would get chips later for our tea. The afternoon passed very pleasantly - nice and sunny. We had some chips around four pm and made our way back to our bikes. Having picked them up we set off for home. As it had taken us roughly four hours to travel from home to Southport we calculated the same going back. Leaving at five pm we reckoned on being home by nine pm. To begin with all was well. We made good progress for the first hour or so but then we began to get tired. We found ourselves wishing we did not have so far to go. We were both dreading the East Lancs Road. It was very dreary cycling along there. I don't know how many miles it was to

Manchester from where we joined it, all I knew was we had to count seven roundabouts before branching off to the left at the seventh. After we left the East Lancs Rd we didn't have a clue where we were except we were on our way to Manchester not far from a place called Prestwich. As we were cycling along at a steady pace, an old man suddenly jumped out at us. He grabbed Elsie's handlebars. She screamed "Get off! Get off! Let go!" but he wouldn't so I took my bicycle pump from its place on the frame of my bike and walloped his hands with it. Whilst he was recovering from this Elsie and I shot off and put some distance between us. That incident put new life in our legs. We knew there was no way he could catch us so after a while we slowed down a little. We next came across a policeman who stopped us to ask questions. Why were we out so late? Where were we going? We told him we were lost and he gave us directions to get to Manchester. We also told him about the man that had jumped out at us. He didn't know what to do with us. Take us to the station for safety or let us go on our way and hope for the best. He let us go on. Another few miles with legs like lead we started to recognise where we were. At last we were no longer lost. When we finally did arrive home our parents were surprised to see us. They thought we were tucked up in a B & B. We had taken enough money to pay for it but everywhere looked full so we had decided not to. I had a key to my house so I could let myself in but Elsie had to knock her parents up. By now it was about two am. We had been on the go for nine hours. No wonder we were shattered. After a nice hot cup of tea, I finally got to bed and slept the following day which fortunately was Sunday. I slept until two pm and did not come round until Monday morning. I decided there and then - no more long distance trips by our two selves. It would have been much better had we had the other club members with us. Things never seem so bad if there are people to share it with. I wondered afterwards if the policeman had got into trouble for leaving two vulnerable young girls out at night on their own.

One weekend it was decided to go camping at a small place near Southport in a farmers' field. Someone with a lorry was taking our camping equipment. We set off on Saturday morning and arrived midday. We pitched camp and then had something to eat and then caught the bus into town. We were all laughing and joking and didn't realise how far we were travelling. We went to the amusements and funfair as usual. We had such a good time we never gave the time a thought until it started to go dark. We had no idea what time the buses ran and stood for ages at a bus stop until some local informed us that the last bus had already departed. Of course, there were no mobile phones then so we were unable to get in touch with anyone to inform them of where we were. It was now quarter to ten at night so we decided we had better start walking. We found it a long, long way back and it didn't help that when we came to a crossroads, we did not know which way to go – left or right. Harry Hall favoured left and Eddie Buck to the right so we just followed whoever we thought was right.

Back at camp though Fred Wallwork and his wife were getting worried about us as by this time it was getting on for midnight. (Their son Kenneth was with us) So Fred got his motorbike out and set off to look for us. I understand there were three ways we could have come back to camp. Fred didn't know which road we would take on the way back from Southport and there was some dissent between us as to which was the correct way. Fred caught up with us eventually and led us back the correct way. What we hadn't realised was the distance from the field in which we had camped to Southport itself because we had gone on the bus in the first instance. Fred clocked the mileage and it was about seven miles. We were shattered when we arrived back and Fred gave us lifts in turn. The four girls all slept in one tent and in the morning we were awakened by the sight of a cow pushing its head through the opening of the tent and going 'MOO" at us. After breakfast we started to decamp and prepare to leave the farm to cycle back to Oldham. We left the equipment for the lorry driver to pick up and off we went back to Chadderton. A few weeks after we had returned the lorry driver had still not brought our equipment back. We spoke to him about it but he was on a different run and wasn't going that way anymore.

Eileen, Elsie and I decided we would go to Southport and bring it back ourselves. We went by train to Ormskirk which was the nearest station to where we had been staying. We found the gear but hadn't thought about how heavy it would be getting it back to the station so we decided to hitch a lift. No-one stopped and just as we were giving up hope a car stopped with some men inside. We girls looked at each other undecided whether or not to get in but the fact that no-one else had stopped and the gear was getting heavier by the minute so we squashed in with them. They smelled of beer and told us they had been to a wedding. We explained about the camping and everything that had transpired and could they drop us off near the station. When we were approaching the station we all panicked a bit wondering if they would let us out but they were good as gold. So, from there we caught the train to Manchester, then one to Oldham then, a bus to Chadderton. That was the one and only time I have ever thumbed a lift.

It was about this time that those with tandems decided they would like to go back to single bikes again. I was one of these. When you have been riding behind someone and seeing nothing but their backside it's no wonder you want the freedom of your own bike. Apart from Harry and Eddie, the rest of us sold our tandems and bought single bikes. Les and I bought one each from a cycle shop on Union St called 'Skidmores' - great name! Soon I had the freedom of the road again. It was harder work than being on the tandem though. Soon afterwards the club began to break up. Harry and his girlfriend Lena got married and gave up cycling altogether. Eddie and his wife had another baby so they had to pack it in. Some of the others started courting people who were not interested in cycling so that was the end of that. I was sorry it broke up but Les and I continued going out on Sundays, both summer and winter, mostly round Derbyshire - so come rain, snow or sun we would be out there. If anyone wanted to come with us, they were welcome but mostly it was just the two of us. Eventually we got engaged and sold our bikes and started saving for the wedding. I must admit I missed those Sundays So that was the end of my cycling days. Good they were, and I would like to re-live them. We did cover the ground in a car a few years ago and although it was nice to travel over hills and dales, Winnat's Pass, Cat and Fiddle, Snake Pass, all these places were quite exciting on a bike but nothing in a car so reliving these days would have to be on a bike. But I am too old for that now worse luck, but others cycle the dales and I hope they get as much pleasure from it as I did all those years ago

Christmas In T'Mill

Christmas has always been an exciting time for me but never more so than when I worked in the cotton mill. It was all very basic and yet somehow there was something both traditional and at the same time spontaneous about it.

First the traditional part. About two weeks before Christmas we would start to trim up with paper decorations – everyone would bring some in and they would be passed around and used on the pillars, posts and walls, but not too close to the machinery. Once the decorations were in place the next tradition was the 'footings'. These took place usually a couple of days before the mill closed down for the Christmas holiday. The reason we had our 'footings' before Christmas and not on the last day of work was so the bosses would let us go home early on breaking up day. Now what are 'footings' I hear you ask. Well, they are a traditional part of Christmas festivities that have occurred in the mill for donkey's years as a way of capturing the Christmas spirit amongst your workmates. And what did 'footings' consist of? Mostly things to eat, especially those we could not normally afford.

The money to pay for all this came from the men. We women (young and old) would chase the men until they were caught and then, with a sprig of mistletoe held over them, they would be well and truly kissed and for the privilege of this they had to pay the woman that had caught them a shilling. With the money the women bought fancy cream cakes, trifles etc from a local confectioner. Also some alcohol to get them in the Christmas Spirit.

In addition to the money collected the women also paid into a kitty – sixpence a week – to raise the funds. It was quite interesting to watch a man racing through the mill with half a dozen women in hot pursuit with a sprig of mistletoe. Sometimes he would get away but if the women all dived on him at once he might as well give up.

For their footings the men usually went to the local pub for a couple of pints of beer- then they would come back to where they normally worked and the women would have saved them some food – after all the men had paid for most of it. Our dinner hour was usually one hour but on 'footings' day the management turned a blind eye and we had at least an hour and a half before re-starting work. It may seem tame to you but we had a good time and lots of laughs, the mill was a close-knit community and things like 'footings' brought us that much closer. You may ask where did the name 'footings' come from? I am not sure but possibly because the men had to foot the bill for the food.

We only had two days break for Christmas – Christmas Day and Boxing Day, and if one of them happened to fall on a Sunday you only got one other day off. That was until the unions stepped in and fought for two days off regardless of the days themselves.

As workers got better off financially they spread their wings somewhat and going out for a meal or visiting the theatre became the norm and 'footings' died out.

Although I enjoyed going to posh restaurants like the Cafe Royal in Manchester, and the Manchester Opera House, to see top stars, somehow it was never the same as those 'footings' where we had sat round the cotton skips with our work mates, and the excitement of chasing someone with the mistletoe. No. There was nothing to touch that.

After The Elk

By the time I was seventeen I was getting bored with yarn testing and wanted something different. One day I saw an ad in the paper for a cashier at the Cafe Monica on Union Street. I had never been inside this place but I did know where it was and I knew it had a reputation of being both expensive and one of the best restaurants in town, so I applied in person, and got the job right away. They told me to come in at nine am the following morning. I think they were pretty desperate by this time. I don't know how long the job had been advertised for but suffice to say I agreed to start the following day after negotiating pay etc. The wages were two pounds and fifteen shillings per week plus lunch and a meal before going home. At the Elk my last wages had been two pounds two shillings and sixpence per week and of course no free meals although the Elk had a very good canteen but all meals had to be paid for. Also having a meal before coming home saved my mother both time and money. The only problem was the hours. I had been used to a straightforward five day week with Saturdays off, but the cafe hours were nine am to two pm – have lunch- then four pm to six pm. The cafe was closed between two and four but there was not enough time to go anywhere or do anything unless one missed out on one's lunch but I enjoyed the job so I stuck it out.

The owner of the cafe – Mrs Gartside – decided to have a bar installed and applied for a licence to sell wines and spirits. The bar did well serving drinks with meals and when I got to be eighteen, I was asked to start working in the bar two or three evenings per week (paid overtime of course) which I did. I enjoyed it, especially on Saturday nights when we had a wedding or a twenty-first birthday party and we were able to join in with the guests. I also got plenty of tips which helped a lot. My duties at the cafe were typing menus, organising functions (including outside catering) funeral parties, and taking cash in the cash kiosk, and totalling up the receipts making sure they tallied with the cash and of course answering the phone. I shared the office with the manager Mr Mills. We had a lovely polished desk each and I had my typewriter on mine. There was a large open coal fire, which was lit in the winter by Albert the porter, who always had it burning brightly by the time Mr Mills and myself arrived. In front of this fireplace was a genuine tiger skin rug and two comfortable armchairs in which we used to sit and drink our morning coffee, and in the afternoon, tea and cakes.

Like everything else one eventually gets fed up with doing the same thing and so came the day when I decided I wanted a change once more and also some more money. After much thinking I came up with the idea of going in the cotton mill only this time I was going to be a winder. So off I went to the Monarch Mill and asked if there were any vacancies for inexperienced winders. I was interviewed by Harry Brooks who was the winding room overlooker. He asked a few questions and took me on, on a month's trial and so I became a winder. This was another job I enjoyed and it was whilst working at the Monarch that I got married to Les on September 10th 1949.

Nora and Les

I must go back a year or two, now to how it came about that I was getting married. I have already stated that I was not interested in Les as a boyfriend, preferring Jack Baynham. Unfortunately, Jack was called up to do his National Service. I corresponded with him for about six months during which time Les was still chasing me. Eventually I gave in and agreed to go on a date with him. Although I still didn't fancy him in that way, he made me laugh and he was a good companion. We went out most nights, to the pictures, and we also started going to Belle Vue Speedway. It was Les's idea in the first place but it was me that became hooked on it in the end and couldn't get enough of it. I really enjoyed it all, the excitement, the atmosphere, the noise, the music. It was similar to the fairground with the same attributes.

Before I had left the Elk Mill a cycling club was started and we started off with eight or ten members (Les and myself included). Les and I got engaged on my nineteenth birthday and married the following September. At first it was going to be a quiet wedding as we were expected to pay for most of it, but then my dad decided he would pay for all of it - but he said he wanted to do the organising. It was decided to hold the reception at the Chadderton Arms which was very close to our abode. The church was St Matthews. Dad invited all the family on my mother's side and all the family on his side, not to mention all those related to Les which as it happened was not all that many. Then there were friends of ours, and friends of Mum and dad etc. In the end I believe the number for the reception was a hundred and fifty plus, and more in the evening. He hired a three-piece band to play for dancing and two tenors to sing – he liked operatic music. As you can imagine we had lots of presents – some were repeated for instance three sets of saucepans, five glass fruit sets, several tablecloths, several pairs of sheets but it was all very much appreciated. All in all, it was a good day and as I thought about it, it seemed a shame that he had spent so much money when I knew there was no way the marriage would last. It just didn't feel right. I think my dad had an inkling of how I was feeling because on the way to the church in the car he said to me 'You don't have to go through with this you know, it's not too late to change your mind and go back.' Believe me I was tempted, but then I thought of all those people waiting for the bride, all the preparations, the presents that would have to be returned. I just couldn't do it even though I wanted to more than anything. Four year later I wished I had been brave enough to do so.

During wartime white weddings were out and in 1949 they were still out so I was married in a blue two piece – very fine wool with gold filigree lace applique on the yoke. My headdress was made up of matching blue feathers and my shoes were grey snakeskin peeptoes and slingbacks, pale blue gloves and a silver horseshoe covered in pink and white freesias and the finest nylons I could fine – 10 denier. The suit was made to measure so it fitted perfectly. Eileen was my bridesmaid and she had a dress of pink trimmed with burgundy velvet ribbon and she looked very nice, Eileen met her future husband at the wedding – Jack Winterbottom. They started going out together almost immediately. They were engaged for two years before they were married. I was most surprised when I heard they were engaged. The Winterbottom family was not considered to be much good. But Jack was different from the rest of them. The older brother Eric was always in trouble – mostly with the police and other authorities. I believe he was in reform school at one time. During my time at the Elk, Eric also worked there but he was always causing trouble. He was always skiving off and being threatened with the sack.

Les and I had already arranged to live at my Grandma's house after we were married. She let us have the front bedroom upstairs but we had to provide our own furniture. We bought a bedroom suite on hire purchase. It was quite expensive – seventy-nine pounds if I remember rightly. This included the wardrobe, dressing tables and chest of drawers, bedside tables and the cost of mattress for the divan bed.

One year after we were married Les decided he wanted to be self employed as a photographer so he bought a plate camera. That was what the professionals went with at the time and set himself up as a roving photographer. By that I mean he didn't have a studio but advertised for work for to travel to i.e. twenty-first birthday parties, weddings etc. Unfortunately, he did not get many replies. As far as I can remember he did one wedding and he also did a nativity play at St Marks school one Christmas. He had left the Elk Mill by now so the only money coming in was what I was earning. My father was furious with him for packing in a good job for something he knew little about and they had a good row. Soon after Les got another job in the mill again but he had to start from the bottom again. Apart from my Dad being furious I wasn't too happy myself. Then Les met up with Tommy Godfrey. Tommy had a second hand furniture shop on Middleton Road next to Tom Enderby's fish and chip shop. We became more and more friendly with Tommy and Tom - they were both musicians and played in the same five piece band so on Saturday nights. We began to go with them to wherever they were playing. That way we got some good nights out for free and when they were playing at a wedding or a party, we joined in that as well. Oh yes, we had some good Saturday nights. We even got some refreshments (sandwiches, cake etc) as well.

Tom and Tommy were now also going out 'scrapping'. That is choosing an area -'billing' it – then going back later that day to collect whatever scrap metal the residents had come up with. This they would load onto Tommy's van, take it back to Oldham to a scrap dealer, weigh it in and divide the profits between them. Needless to say, they paid the people who brought out the scrap to them but obviously at a lower price than they would get from the scrap dealer. Tommy suggested to Les that as he wasn't earning much then he join them in their quest for more scrap. That way they could cover a larger area and hopefully earn more money. Les agreed to this, although I myself wasn't too sure about this arrangement. But I didn't have much choice. Soon afterwards Ray (my future second husband!) also joined 'the firm' so now there was four of them covering a much larger area. Apparently one of the best places to collect was in the Cheshire area of Northwich.

Tommy got in trouble with the Police and they practically ran him out of town. As he was dealing in scrap metal some of the chaps who worked at Platts across the road were bringing gun metal ingots to sell. These were not scrap at all, but stolen. One day he got a tip off that his premises was about to be raided that night. He knew he had some ingots there and if the police turned up, they would be found so he had to get rid of them quick. Tommy came down to my Grandma's house and spoke to Les on the doorstep. I didn't know what was going on at that time but it seemed he wanted Les to help dispose of them. The ingots being heavy were still on Tommy's premises. Les agreed to help so they went back to Tommy's place and loaded them in Tommy's van all the while looking over their shoulder for any sign of police activity. Fortunately, there was none. If only the Police had known what was happening at that time! Tommy asked Tom Enderby to help as well but although he was happy enough to take his share of the money when the lads from Platts sold Tommy the ingots, he wouldn't have anything to do with their disposal. Once they had got the van loaded Tommy and Les set off for Hollingworth Lake which was a few miles away from

Oldham and dumped them all in the lake. I don't know if they were ever found. It would only be if the lake ever dried up would they be found. As it turned out the police did not raid Tommy's premises that night - something else turned up they had to deal with so all was well. But every time Tommy went out playing in the band on a Saturday night, they would be waiting for him outside his property looking inside the van. Naturally he got fed up with this so he made up his mind to sell up and leave Oldham.

A move to The Isle of Wight

Tommy Godfrey had been to the Isle of Wight beforehand, both as a holidaymaker when he took all his family, and on his own when he got a job playing in a band there. On this occasion he had stayed at a house in Victoria Road with the Webber family – Gordon Webber also being in this band. He felt sure that the Webbers would be willing to put him up again if he moved down to the Island. He did not want to go on his own so he asked Les if he fancied going as well. As you can imagine Les was in favour of this and arranged to go down there and see what the job situation was like.. Tommy knew a chap down there – Ken Mills – who was also a musician and had a good job at Saunders-Roe and he agreed to test the water for them. To cut a long story short they got an interview with the personnel manager who agreed they could start work but they would have to go to the apprentices training school first to learn the basic skills necessary to become semi-skilled operatives. To start with though they had to do labouring jobs until there were vacancies. Next thing they had to do when they got back to Oldham was talk me into agreeing to go and live on the Island. This they did by filling me up with alcohol until I had weakened. Once I had made up my mind to go, I started to look forward to my adventure, even though I knew my parents were not going to be too happy about it. After the row there had been over the photography interlude, I was not looking forward to telling them I was moving to the Isle of Wight. I tried to soften the blow by suggesting that once we had got established, they would be able to come for holidays and to think of the money it would save them. So, we did move to the island but Tommy's wife Nellie and their six children were unable to come down straightaway so myself, Les and Tommy all stayed at Mrs Webbers place.

Tommy's shop had to go up for sale so it needed someone to stay in Oldham and oversee this. Once the shop was sold Tommy could then look for a house for his own family. He chose Cowes. He had already hit on one that he fancied. It was quite big, an old Victorian property with four bedrooms, two large rooms downstairs, bathroom, large kitchen, washhouse, small front garden and large back garden. I think the price was in the region of four thousand pounds. He did not get much for the shop in Oldham so he had to have a large mortgage. He worked all the overtime he could in order to earn the sort of money necessary to warrant a mortgage of that size.

We travelled to the Island in Tommy's van. He fixed it up inside with two large armchairs out of a three-piece suite and very comfortable it was too. I nearly forgot to mention that Nellie's father came with us. He travelled in the back of the van with me whilst Les sat in the front with Tommy. Whilst we were in Southampton waiting for the ferry it was decided to go into the pub for a drink and give us a chance to have a wash and brush up. Unfortunately, when we came back, we found some of the suitcases were missing – one of mine, one of Les's, and one belonging to Nellie's father. Mine had my post office saving account book in it with a hundred and twenty pounds in the account so we had to sort that out very quickly. The rest of the stuff was new clothes I had bought for my new life. We got the late night ferry eventually and arrived in Cowes early morning. The post office soon sorted out the missing book and we did not lose any of our money so all was well in the end. I was quite surprised to see how popular Tommy was with the Webbers. They thought he was marvellous or at least that was how it seemed to me.

When we had been on the Island a couple of weeks, we decided it was time we started to look for a house for ourselves. There was an ad in the local paper: Seventeen shillings and six pence will buy you a house in Cowes, then five shillings a week (sellers stood the mortgage themselves in those days) plus rates (now the council tax) so we thought we had better follow this up. It seemed too good to be true. It was a box number and turned out to be 36 York St. The house had two rooms downstairs, four bedrooms but no bathroom and a basement kitchen and an outside toilet which was next to the kitchen but could not be reached by going through the kitchen, only by going out of the back door. The garden at the back was quite large and had blackcurrant bushes, gooseberry bushes, raspberries and blackberries. We decided it would do us at least until we could afford something better. I always had my eye on Ward Avenue as the place I would most like to live but I never got there. There was just one time when we could have afforded it but I will get round to that later.

In order to afford it I needed to get a job and add to the income of Les and myself. I applied for one or two jobs advertised in the local paper but I was not suitable. One night Les and I were in the Globe Hotel on the seafront in Cowes and who should come in but Mr Gillespie from Saunders-Roe. He knew Les of course from interviewing him for the job he now had. But he did not know me. We got talking and he asked how the job seeking was progressing. I told him I was not having much success and he asked what kind of jobs I had been applying for and what kind of job I had been doing in Oldham before coming to the Island. When I explained I had been a cotton operative he asked if I would be willing to work on the factory floor here in Cowes. I said yes, I would be very willing. He said no more after that – bought us both a drink and then left. The following Thursday when I went to the labour exchange to collect my unemployment benefit there was a message for me - would I go to see Mr. Clark at Saunders Roe that same afternoon, which I did, and was informed I could start work the following Monday if I wished. The wage was five pounds and fifteen shillings plus bonus. This was marvellous because when I left the Monarch mill my wage was only four pounds and ten shillings. This was a twenty-five per cent increase in income. I was over the moon as you can imagine. Les was soon on ten pounds per week and what with my wages we were doing very well financially.

    I enjoyed the job and the company and my mum and dad came down to the Island three years running, bringing with them their friends Joe and Annie Smith. They all enjoyed their stay there. They always came in Royton wakes week which was last week of July / first week in August which happened to coincide with Cowes week on the island. They didn't understand the first thing about yachting, any more than I did but they loved the atmosphere. I was very happy both in my job and in my friends. My great friend was 'Midge', or Margaret, as she was actually called. We went to play darts together, also practiced together. May and Eli (Les's parents) fancied moving from Oldham to the island so Eli came first and stayed with us at our house. Whilst he was there a friend of Tommy's also came to the Island. He had nowhere to stay as Tommy's house was full up (they were taking in B and B) so they asked if I could take him in. After all that Tommy had done for us I could hardly refuse so that is how Jimmy Chadwick came into our lives. Both Eli and Jimmy had a good sense of humour and we had some great times with them both. I did the cooking but I never washed a pot. Jimmy and Eli always ended up arguing, in fun, who was going to do it. Both Jimmy and Eli started to look for a house to buy and Eli found one in Stanley Road, Cowes and Jimmy one in East Cowes.

Jimmy had a wife called Mattie, short for Matilda, and they had two children, a girl called Gillian and a boy called Stewart. May and Eli of course had a daughter Marjorie, a daughter Sheila (with whom I became close friends) and a son Kenneth. Both Eli and Jimmy got labouring jobs to start off with and then later became semi-skilled workers. Later on, they both left to take up different types of employment – Eli became a brewery warehouse manager and Jimmy to do a driving job. Marjorie decided to take up nursing which she did at St Mary's hospital but she did not stay long. I think it was too heavy work for her. She was only little and some of the patients were quite heavy.

When we had been on the island a couple of years Les got the hankering to go back to Oldham. I was quite happy to stay as we were but I could see Les wanted to sell the house and with the extra money buy a car. We did buy one at one time but you never saw anything like it. It was about twenty years old and the tyres were so thin every time we went out in it we never got any further than the bottom of the street before 'bang!' - another puncture. Fortunately for us, Sammy Williams garage was in the middle of the street so we could always leave the wheel there for him to repair whilst Les changed the spare. It got to the stage eventually when I wouldn't go anywhere in it in case of breakdowns. Punctures weren't the only thing. One summer when George Driver (who was a sergeant at Chadderton police station) and his wife Annie and their two children came to stay with us. We loaned them the car to use whilst we were working. Annie had to sit in the back and hold on to both doors to stop them flying open. It should have been a very comfortable car, the back seat was an air cushion and could be blown up, but even that was punctured and never stayed up long. It was so big and ugly and noisy. Like a great big tank lumbering along and I was never so happy as the day we finally got rid of it. We sold it to three university students for a tenner, we having paid twenty pounds for it originally, not counting the cost of numerous five shilling puncture repairs.

I have not mentioned any of the financial problems on the Island. I had a habit of putting money away to pay the bills as they became due, I put this money aside religiously. But too often when I came to want the money to pay the bill it was missing and I had to try to get it all back together again before the due date. We had many rows about this as you can imagine. In the end I decided I would have to split up with Les before we got into debt. Les's answer to problems of this nature was to borrow and I am sure we would have finished up thousands in debt if it had been left to him.

After the episode with the car Les bought a motor bike, A Royal Enfield 350 cc. I think he gave twenty pounds for it. I used to ride pillion and I enjoyed the bike better than the old car. Even that could be very temperamental for starting though. One summer evening we decided to go across to Freshwater and when we arrived there, we switched off the engine and sat on the grass taking in the evening sunshine. When we decided to set off back home the bike wouldn't start no matter how much Les tried to kick start it. It wasn't having any. Whilst we were struggling who should come along but two cops on bikes.

"Having trouble?" one said. "Let me see what I can do. I used to be a speedway rider before I joined the police" I had other things to worry about at that time as we had no taxation or insurance. There were no MOT's then otherwise we would not have had that either. This copper must have been so engrossed in the bike he never asked for proof of insurance or notice the absence of a taxation disc. He never did manage to get it to start so we got away from him as soon as we were able. Needless to say, we sorted out the insurance and taxation the following Monday.

When we bought the house, it cost six hundred and fifty pounds and we sold it for seven hundred and seventy–five pounds minus legal fees. We had done a lot to it. We modernised the kitchen and toilet and put in a new tiled fireplace which cost twelve pounds which I paid for by giving up smoking for six weeks. Tommy had helped us with the decorating. It looked very nice when it was finished. As we had no home of our own to go to we asked if we could go back home to my mother's house. They had no room for our furniture so we had to sell most of that as well. We put a postcard in a local window to advertise it. A dining suite, a bedroom suite, a bed settee and a gas cooker. I can't remember how much we got for it but the owners of the shop we put the advert in came along to have a look and bought it al'' en bloc'. They wanted to buy the piano as well but I had to explain that it belonged to my father so I wasn't at liberty to sell it. I think the total would have been about a hundred pounds. We now had a total of two hundred and twenty-five pounds and Les saw a car advertised for a hundred and twenty-five pounds. He offered a hundred and fifteen and this was accepted and so we had our first decent car. We drove back to Oldham in the car which was a Morris 12. Mind you we had no home of our own but our name was still down on the council housing list. We went back to live at my parents' house. I don't think my grandparents wanted the upheaval of having us there again. I put the balance of the money in a Post Office account in my name so Les couldn't get at it, but eventually he had it off me bit by bit. It wasn't long before I had had enough of Les and so once I met up with Ray again it was all over. We will now go on to the time Ray and I left Oldham to make a new life down in Somerset.

Wedding day of Nora and Les

Big George, Sarah Ann, Les, Nora, Annie, Little George

Nora and Ray

Farm Work

When I got back to Oldham and met up with Ray once more, I could see he was the right one for me. And so we decided to move away from Oldham.

Ray having had the experience of working and living on the farm explained it all to me and I agreed with him that we should move on to Somerset or Wiltshire. Ray had a small Bedford flat bottom lorry open to the weather. He also had some furniture he was going to sell but he decided instead to take it with us. If we got a job with a tied cottage, we would need furniture. We didn't expect to get a furnished place. It was arranged that Ray would load up the Bedford and then pick me up from Park View. This would be at a time when I was the only one in the house, both my parents and Les being at work. I had already given in my notice and collected my wages and holiday pay to take with us. We drove first of all to Warminster and stayed at a hotel there. I think it was the King's Arms, right in the centre of town. We had B & B and the next morning set off looking for work. We bought a local paper – the Western Gazette and went through the vacancies column concentrating on the jobs of farm labourer which offered a tied cottage. The first one Ray was turned away from due to lack of experience but the second farmer he went to see was in Kilmington and he must have been desperate because he took him on without too many questions being asked.

The farmer showed us the cottage which was very basic although it had a thatched roof – very picturesque from the outside but a bit bleak inside. There was no electricity or gas, but there was running water, but no hot water system – only cold water, No bathroom obviously but a big tin bath in the kitchen. It would have taken many, many bucketfuls of water to fill it. Also, there was no plug to empty it if you ever got it full. Consequently, we did not use it preferring a stand up wash at the kitchen sink. We had a kettle on the range which was our only way of heating water and it took ages to boil. The cottage had real beams which gave it a more genuine look. I couldn't keep managing on the range so we had to go to a shop in Mere and buy a primus stove and a special box to use for cooking. One placed the box on top of the primus stove, closed the door and it was just like an oven. I made some lovely pies in it. I was quite surprised how good they turned out. For boiling, like potatoes or other veg, that was done directly on the primus. It was a lot quicker boiling water for tea on the primus than it was on the range. The cottage had a very large garden, three bedrooms, one downstairs room (where the fireplace was) and a kitchen. As we had so little furniture and could not afford to buy any, not even second hand, the rooms looked very bare. We paid no rent for the cottage, got free milk, and were paid seven pounds a week with two pounds extra at harvest time when the haymaking was done.

As I have already stated there was a very large garden but for Ray there was no time to make full use of it. We did grow some lettuces during the summer months but we put too many in at one go and were overloaded with them and finished up having to give most of them to the rabbits in the next field. There was an outside toilet consisting of an Elsan can, the contents of which are buried in the garden. Chemicals are placed in the can to breakdown the contents and the whole thing is placed inside a small shed.

There was only one street in the village and the main shop was at the top – the opposite end to where we lived. This shop sold just about everything and had a post office. The only thing it did not sell was meat, but there was a butcher's van came round twice a week and stopped at various points in the street. Also, there was a baker's van and a hardware van which sold paraffin (a vital ingredient) and a greengrocery van, so as you can see, practically everything was covered. Apart from visiting Kilmington these travelling vans also went over the Deverills, a collection of little villages in the Longleat and Warminster area. It was a great area for growing plants and suchlike. Very fertile soil. Stourhead is not very far away and some of the roses growing around there are nearly as big as cabbages. Of course, everything has changed now. Last time I was there I hardly recognised the place. I certainly could not locate where our cottage was. Oh, the other thing I should have mentioned. We had to share the cottage with some livestock during the first few days ... fleas. So it was down to the shop in Mere once again. This time for flea powder. After that Ray was always washing to make sure he did not bring any home from the farm.

One day Ray came home carrying a little white kitten. He had rescued it from being trampled by the cows. The farmer and the rest of the workforce did not take any notice of it. To them the poor thing had to look out for itself and if it couldn't...well... but Ray being soft about animals (and why not) couldn't bear to see it trampled to death so he dived in amongst the cows, picked it up and put it somewhere safe until it was time to come home. The rest of them thought he was mad for going to all that trouble but Ray knew I would be pleased. We called her Tiddles and she was a lovely cat.

It was May when we took up residence in Kilmington and the first week we had snow. Can you believe it? Afterwards though we had a beautiful summer, lots of sunshine, and hot weather.

We were fortunate in having that Bedford van. It was our lifeline with the outside world. There were no bus services except one every Tuesday to Salisbury for the market and one every Christmas to Manchester, so the old Bedford came in handy to take us to the pictures on a Saturday night. We had a choice of three – Frome, Warminster or Gillingham. We used to buy the Western Gazette and choose which film we fancied seeing.

Before we went, we would spend some time rolling cigarettes, about twenty, and place them in a tin. These were then ready to smoke in the cinema. This was of course because we could not afford to buy the real thing, except on special occasions, even though cigarettes were so much cheaper than today. Still, we saved on one thing - there were no parking charges in car parks.

We couldn't go very far on a Sunday. Ray had to be there in the morning for the milking and if we were to go anywhere, we always had to be back for the four pm milking so you can see how it was. However, he was allowed a week off for holidays after the morning milking was done so we managed to go places that week. We went to Wells, West Bay and Bath and other places I can't remember but I know we had a lovely week.

We had a good look round Frome as we had only seen it form the cinema car park before, so we looked round the town itself and the shops. There were quite a few antique and second hand shops there which was interesting and there was a church. which, when the clock struck the hour and the quarters, played 'Oh God our help in ages past' - one line from the hymn on each quarter.

We spent one Christmas there in Kilmington all on our own. We didn't drink in those days but on Christmas Eve we decided that after visiting the cinema we would call in the pub on the way home. The one we chose was called the Cross Keys and what a place it was.

I don't know if we chose the wrong room because as we entered there was no-one there at all, but there was a bar with a hatch that one knocked on to get service. This we did, got served, and then the barman shut the hatch in our faces. Needless to say, we never went in that pub again. One day we will go back to see if it is still the same.

We had a very cold Christmas, not having enough wood to keep the fire going properly and not being able to afford coal for a hot fire. We decided we would not be able to stand another winter under those circumstances plus we needed more money coming in. We needed somewhere I could get a job as well and then we would have two wages. We looked through the local paper to see if there were any houses to rent but nothing doing. All the houses in there were for sale for about four hundred pounds and they wanted cash.

We put an ad in there ourselves asking for anyone offering rented accommodation. We got a few replies offering caravan accommodation. One of these was positioned in West Coker which was close to Yeovil. We decided to accept this one. We thought being close to Yeovil it would be the best for jobs.

The caravan was in the middle of a field next to a farm. There was a tap in the field from which we got our water. It was quite a small caravan but there was also another building next to the caravan, almost like a chalet, so we set the bed up there and just used the caravan for eating and cooking.

We took the cat Tiddles with us of course. I believe she enjoyed it there more than Kilmington. Once we got ourselves established, we enjoyed it there.

Ray went to the local labour exchange looking for work and right away he got taken on at Merriott mouldings. I got a job at Westland helicopters so we were both happy.

The rent for the caravan was one pound fifteen shillings a week which after living rent free for so long seemed quite a lot, but out of our combined wages wasn't so bad.

Working at Westland for me was very similar to being at Saunders-Roe. I liked being amongst planes. We now had a change of cinema to visit in Yeovil but we still didn't go drinking on Saturday nights – just the cinema.

Back to Oldham

All during the time I had been away from Oldham I had been in touch with Mum and Dad by writing to them but I never put our address on the letter. I posted them in various places, usually when we went to the pictures. I didn't want them to know where I was in case they told Les, should he turn up wanting to know about us. However, one day I slipped up. I let it be known I had bought a two-piece suit from John Colliers. My mother did some detective work and traced us to Yeovil so one day I came home from work and found her and my dad waiting for us by the caravan. We had a good discussion and finally they persuaded us to go back to Oldham. They looked out for a house for us to buy, a four roomed terrace type, with its own back yard and outside toilet for three hundred and fifty pounds - fifty pounds deposit and a pound a week (sellers stood the mortgage themselves in those days). We didn't have the deposit but my dad lent it to us and so we arrived back in Oldham once more.

This time Ray went to the Werneth Mill which was almost opposite our house and I went to the GEC in Shaw. We were right on the bus route for Shaw. The bus stop was directly opposite our house.

The money was better than the farm and my wage was better than Yeovil although Ray's wasn't much different to Merriott mouldings at Crewkerne. We had a better lifestyle back in Oldham and started to go out for a drink now and then as well as still going to the pictures. In Oldham there was a much larger choice of cinemas to visit and we didn't need to rely so much on the old Bedford. Everywhere was on a bus route and cheap at that.

After a while working at the Werneth Mill, Ray applied for a job at Dennis Ferranti's working on electrical transformers. He did this for some time and then he was asked to start going out to jobs to 'rectify', in North Wales.

A Trip to Scotland

Ray was working at Denis Ferranti's when he was asked to take a lorry full of stuff up to Morar in Scotland for the Ferranti estate.

The first trip he went on was with another employee, someone to share the driving with as it was a four hundred mile journey from Oldham. The second time they were asked to do the journey the other fellow refused to go. Ray didn't fancy going on his own so he came back home and asked me if I would like to go. Obviously, I couldn't help with the driving but it was the company he wanted as much as anything. Four hundred miles is a long way on your own with no-one to talk to. Of course, I said yes right away. This was in January by the way, one of the coldest months of the year especially in Scotland. So, the following morning I donned my winter woollies and my fur coat, climbed aboard the cab of the lorry and we set off. Our first stop was Shap Fell. This is in Cumbria. On that particular day it was covered in snow and very picturesque it looked with the mountains in the background, standing out with their snowy peaks rising high above the town itself. Shap as it is better known, has a steep road leading out of it and in the winter time when the road becomes snowed up and icy, hundreds of lorries get stranded when the drivers have to abandon their vehicles and leave them until the snow and ice melt. Fortunately for us it was not so on this day.

After stopping at a lovely cafe for a cup of tea etc we continued on our journey. After Shap, the next place of any note that we came to was Carlisle, and then Glasgow. We didn't stop in either of these places, too busy, but waited until we found a transport cafe on the outskirts of Carlisle and had something to eat and drink before moving on.

We then came to Gretna Green, a place where couples under twenty-one could be married without parents' consent. It was a blacksmiths forge, and the marriage took place 'over the anvil'. It was well-known for under age marriages. We did not stop to have a look around, we didn't have the time. Needless to say, it is no longer possible to marry there. I don't know when it became illegal to marry there. Originally, it was some ancient Scottish Law going back some hundreds of years that had never been repealed, but eventually the twentieth century caught up. After Gretna Green our next port of call was Corpach. By this time the weather had become very cold and we came across a pub. We decided to stop and get a drink. When we entered the pub, I found there were no women inside, just men stood in a circle round the bar. When they spotted Ray and myself, they made a pathway up to the bar. "Give this young lady whatever she wants' said one man who appeared to be in charge, so as I wanted to get warm I asked for a rum and blackcurrant. I was offered another one but one was enough. I could feel it taking hold of me. Ray had a half of beer. It seemed they were celebrating the New Year. This was in the middle of January. We thanked them for their hospitality and went on our way feeling on top of the world.

After leaving Corpach our next road was the one to Morar itself, and what a road that was. It was full of potholes, enormous ones at that, and also the road was very narrow. It took Ray all his time to keep the lorry on a straight path. There was ten miles of this road and it took the best part of four hours to cover it. What I found as we passed several lochs on the way was the very fine white sand of the shoreline. It was almost tropical, you couldn't believe you were in Scotland. By the time we arrived in Morar it was evening and snowing, time to start looking for a place to stay the night. The first place we tried was full and so was the second. I was beginning to get worried we might have to sleep in the cab. Someone suggested we go down to Mallaig, a few miles away, and try the hotel down there. By this time, we were cold and wet and I think I was in tears. When we arrived at

Mallaig the first hotel we tried had a room so I cheered up knowing I would be sleeping in a comfortable bed. We had a good night's sleep and when we awoke the following morning the sun was streaming in through the window. I got out of bed and looked out of the window. The scene was reminiscent of Brixham harbour. Mallaig is a fishing port as well as being where the ferries leave for the Western Isles like the Isle of Skye, which could be seen in the distance. Taken all round it was a lovely scene which opened up in front of us.

When we had first arrived at the hotel, we had Scottish beef for dinner. For breakfast, we had the usual porridge followed by a full Scottish Breakfast. It was a lovely hotel and we decided to re-book for the return journey. After this we settled the bill and continued on our way to Loch Morar. It was a beautiful sunny day, just like Spring, it was hard to believe it was still only January. A boat came over from the other side of the loch, that was where Dennis Ferranti's estate was, and the items we had brought up from Oldham were loaded onto it. Once everything was off, we could start to make our way back home again. To begin with it was a nice journey, lovely sunshine as I have mentioned, and something I had never thought I would see in reality. Imagine the picture 'Monarch of the Glen' - the original is a Victorian painting by George Stubbs. It shows a stag with very large antlers stood high on a rocky ledge, surveying the land around him. As we turned a bend in the road, the same road with all the potholes, there he was high up in front of us, exactly as in the painting. It took my breath away to see in reality what I had only ever seen in a painting. It was a wonderful sight, one that I have never forgotten and never will.

As I have mentioned previously the day started off well with bright spring sunshine, but as the day wore on and we approached Loch Lomond, the weather began to turn nasty. It was necessary to travel through Glencoe, a place in the hills, where in the eighteenth century there was a massacre by one clan. I think it was the Campbells against another clan.

Glencoe is noted for bad weather in the winter time - lots of snow and blizzards, and that's just what we encountered as we entered the area. The snow was coming down thick and fast and blizzard conditions began to take hold. I have experienced blizzards in Oldham but compared to a blizzard in Scotland, especially in Glencoe, they are nothing like the same. What made matters worse the lorry only had one windscreen wiper which was of course on the driver's side. Even so, Ray had to keep stopping to clear the windscreen. It couldn't keep up with the amount of snow falling on the windscreen. As for me I couldn't see a thing, my half of the windscreen was completely covered, making me in effect blind. That's a journey I'm not likely to forget again either.

However, as we started to descend into the valley the snow began to turn to rain and washed the windscreen and generally made driving conditions a bit easier. I could see where I was going at last. It was a good thing we had booked into the hotel that night as a lot of people were hoping to break the journey at the hotel due to the atrocious weather conditions. Some had to be turned away. That could have been us if we had not pre-booked.

After another wonderful dinner of fresh salmon from the loch we sat by a roaring fire in deep armchairs. I should say that although the hotel was not centrally heated we were provided with three hot water bottles for our bed. We had another good sleep and a filled our tummies with the breakfast and then set off to return home, passing through Fort William. I needed the toilet but after getting out at a cafe I found the toilets were frozen so I could not use them. Further on, there were some public conveniences which were still usable. So I went in these. My nose turned red as soon as I got out of the cab, Inside, I found four young girls with a radio, they were listening to music and dancing. Maybe there were no proper dance halls in Fort William so they had to do their dancing in the toilets? I think Fort William must be one of the coldest places in the country in winter.

The remainder of the journey was uneventful. We made good time only stopping once for tea and a meal in a transport cafe and arrived home in the late evening around ten-thirty pm. After sitting in the cab for so long we were stiff when we got home. The house was cold and bleak after having no fire lit for several days so we made hot water bottles and went to bed. We woke the following day feeling tired, but once we had got a fire going we were able to look back at our weekend away with exhilaration.

There is a postscript to this little tale that came two days later in the shape of a local police sergeant. He wanted to know if Ray was the driver of a lorry belonging to Dennis Ferranti's firm and if he had been driving it on a certain day in North Wales. A lorry of that description and with that number plate had been involved in an accident there, on the same day we were in Morar. Ray explained that yes, he had been driving the lorry on that day, but in Scotland, and not in Wales. As it happened, we still had the hotel bills to verify this statement, plus we suggested the Police get in touch with Denis Ferranti who could vouch for Ray being there. Some member of the public had given the wrong vehicle registration to the Police who naturally chased it up. After seeing the hotel bills and hearing our explanation of events the Sergeant seemed to be satisfied and accepted a few whiskies before leaving. I expected him to refuse, saying he was on duty, but he didn't. Perhaps he was still in New Year mode. Whatever the reason we never heard any more about it. We have never been back to Scotland since that week-end. We would have liked to and many times said we would one day but the day never came and now it's too late. At least I can remember those few days in my mind by putting pen to paper.

After Ferranti's

Ray enjoyed working for Dennis Ferranti, away from the factory, but of course the job had to come to an end eventually, and he did not like the idea of going back to work in the factory again, so he bought a bigger lorry and started up a carrying business (man and van!) but he had to be careful because he did not have a licence to do it. He did apply for one but was refused, but he carried on by going to the salerooms and working for the dealers who didn't have their own transport and he earned a living that way.

By this time I had left GEC and gone to work at Ferranti's in Hollinwood. I did not like it there so went to a mail order company where it was mostly working with figures. I did well there, making a good bonus. In January 1961 I got a phone call whilst I was at work that my husband Leslie Smith had been killed in a motorcycle accident on the Isle of Wight. He had returned to the Island and had been living with May and Eli after he and I had split up. So the next day Ray and I went down to the Island on the train. We rang Tommy to let him know we were coming and he met us at Ryde Pier and took us back to the chip shop and put us up. They lived above the chip shop so had plenty of room. They put us up for a few days whilst we held the funeral. As there was no crematorium on the Island at that time we had to go on the ferry from Cowes to Southampton.

We set up in business

After the funeral Ray and I went back to Oldham and I had some insurance money to come from a policy I had taken out when Les and I were first married. It amounted to somewhere in the region of five hundred pounds. We had already booked a holiday in Bournemouth so that was paid for out of the insurance money with some left over. That was when it was decided to use the rest of the money to get started in the second hand business. I became pregnant in July of 1961 and we found a shop for sale advertised in the Oldham Chronicle round about August and we moved in November. We had a terrible winter. You were born in March and on the day you came home it snowed about four inches deep. Before that the weather had been terrible – ice and snow on the roads, freezing fog, smog, that was all outside. Inside wasn't much better. We had no coal for the fire and couldn't afford to buy any. When we first started we didn't do too badly with quite a few customers but when the weather turned really nasty no-one came out looking for furniture. It was all they could do to go out for essentials. One week the only profit made amounted to eight shillings and four pence. One of Ray's former schoolmates, who was a joiner came along and asked Ray if he would do some driving for him for a couple of days which helped the money situation. Fortunately when we bought the shop we only had to put two hundred and fifty pounds deposit down and were paying off the rest at two pounds per week so we still had some capital left although most of it had gone on buying stock. Nevertheless, the bills kept mounting up. It was a good thing when spring arrived, the weather changed and customers started to come round again. I started to advertise in the Oldham Chronicle and from then on things started to get better financially.

    Do you remember the shop on Ashton Road? You spent most of your time at your Grandma's house in Park View. This was because I had to spend most of my time in the shop and couldn't give you the time to look after you properly. Your grandma was able to take you out in the pushchair. You may ask why your dad couldn't take over from me but he needed to go to the salerooms almost every day. So I had to stay in the shop. I must confess I hated it and was always pleased when he got back and I could leave. Once I had learned to drive and we had a car as well as the van I could go down to Park View and pick you up and bring you home. Sometimes if we were early we would call at Auntie Marian's so you could play with Gina for a while. From the shop you went to Hathershaw school and you did very well there. Although I did not like being in the shop there were some funny moments. For example we had a boy's bike in the shop and a woman came in to look at it with a view to buying it for her son. We were discussing the size and she asked me if I thought it would suit him as he was not very tall but had size six shoes. What was I supposed to deduce from that? Another strange remark was when we had an electric cooker in the shop. It was marked up at six pounds and one chap came in and had a good look at it. He then left the shop but turned and said 'If that had been a fridge I would have had it!" Also, the number of people who ask for chairs and then you show them a set of four dining chairs (about ten pounds) and they say they only want one. What they mean is have you got anything really cheap – their explanation being 'it's only for sitting on' or if they wanted money discounted off a cot they'd say 'it's only for a baby'. We knew what they meant though. They wanted something cheap but when they were shown something cheap it wasn't cheap enough! We had some people who came in the shop that we nicknamed TW's - Time-wasters. People who were enquiring for their 'friend' or sister or brother and promised to tell the said person all about it. Usually the most expensive item in the shop. The minute they went down this route we knew they were TW's and gave up on them.

    Once we had paid off the shop, we looked around for a house so we could move out of the shop and all the living accommodation could be used for stock. Thus, giving us more selling space and more money! We bought a house in Royton, Lynton Ave and you changed schools to go to Royton Primary.

It wasn't many years after this that my mother died of kidney failure. According to the doctors it was brought on by too many pills particularly aspirin which she had been prescribed for her arthritis. Nowadays they know better and have other medication for the pain and inflammation so the problem of kidney failure does not arise. She was only sixty-six when she died and soon afterwards we moved to Bournemouth. Originally, we intended moving to the Isle of Wight but because Flo and Bill were in Bournemouth your Dad decided to give Bournemouth a try. Later on, I was glad we had moved to Bournemouth as although I love the Island, I realised it would have been too restrictive having to travel by ferry every time you wanted to go anywhere on the mainland. So, in the end I settled for Bournemouth and we have been here ever since.

Nora at Isle of Wight

Ivy, Annie, Nora, Ray, and George

Bournemouth

We moved to Bournemouth and moved into 16 St James's Square in December 1969. Neville, Ray and Bill took on a shop between them on Christchurch Road, Pokesdown. Not far from the station. It was during this period that Bill had his heart attack and died. After this Ray got the idea in his head he wanted to go back to Oldham and open another shop up there. Which he did. In Hollinwood. He kept this up for a while, coming down on alternate weekends whilst I was doing Bed and Breakfast during the summer months. Neither of these ventures paid off and eventually we had to call it a day. I had to get a job, which I did at Cavendish Rentaflora, washing artificial flowers used in floral displays for hotels and businesss, and Ray got a job at Kennedy's builders merchants. After that we never looked back. Every Saturday night we went to the Hotel Waters Edge disco and also went there on Sunday nights dancing and listening to Chris Conrad who played the organ. There was always lots of holidaymakers in as it was an hotel so the ambience was always good.

We carried on this lifestyle until I bought a lease on a small cafe in Parkwood Road. The main customers where antique dealers from round about. They used it as a meeting place. In addition to the dealers were builders and scaffolders. After a couple of years cooking I had enough and so we changed it over to a second hand and antiques business and later on put it on the market and sold it to Duncan Lloyd. Ray now gave up his job at Kennedys and started pine stripping instead. He fixed up a large tank in the shed in the backyard and carried it on from there.

When we moved to Stourvale Road in March 1985, it came with us.

I didn't give up on the antiques trade straightaway. I took a pitch in the local antiques market and it was during this time that I found I had cancer so I decided it was time to give it up altogether. In 1984 I was diagnosed with breast cancer and had a mastectomy operation after which I had five weeks of radiotherapy. I was okay for many years after that until 2002 when I became ill and had to go to hospital as the tumours have returned. I am now on all sorts of tablets, I think it's twelve a day at present and I can feel myself deteriorating as the years pass by. When your dad was seventy he had prostate cancer. Fortunately, I was still fit at the time. I couldn't cope now. Thankfully he recovered from it and he has been okay since, touch wood.

Since 2002 I haven't done anything very much and now here I am writing this family history which I hope someone is going to read. The date is 7th June 2004 and I am now seventy-four...

I hope to have a holiday on the Island this summer but I think it will be my last. I don't feel I will be fit enough after that.

I have three grandchildren – Roxanne, Jason and Daniel. At the time of writing Roxanne is nineteen and working in a day nursery. Jason is eighteen and at Brockenhurst College studying art and design, and Daniel is sixteen and leaves school this year and will go to Brockenhurst to study Public Services.

I have been wondering if Roxanne will choose a career or will she decide to have children. If she decides to have children I will be very disappointed if I miss out on seeing them, especially as babies. However there is nothing I can do about that. It is Roxanne's choice. Either way, a career or family, I wish her the best of luck for the future. If she chooses a family I hope she will have a good few years beforehand enjoying life and the freedom of a childfree responsibility.

I think I will let someone else continue the story from here. Thank you for reading about me and I wish you good health.

Nora

Nora passed away on 21 November 2005 aged seventy-five

Lightning Source UK Ltd.
Milton Keynes UK
UKHW021836230220
359192UK00013B/318

9 780244 773496